A GUIDE TO
THE WORLD OF
HIGH SCHOOL
TRIGONOMETRY

Table of Contents

Table of Contents

Table of Contents

Message From the Author

Thank you for purchasing this book and welcome to high school trigonometry!

This guide is a great companion for sharpening existing trigonometric skills and learning new ones. In this book, you will be able to extend your knowledge from Algebra 1 and Geometry by interacting with triangles, graphical representations, ratios, identities, and so much more.

In each lesson, read the content and make sure to play close attention at the samples, graphs, and diagrams. Also, look at the embedded tips and notes since they highlight key ideas to remember. Then, check your understanding by completing the practice problems.

Now let's explore this fascinating world of trigonometry and dive right into it!

~ *Raman Arora*

Unit

1

Properties of Triangles

1.1 Similar Triangles

The basis of trigonometry originated from the idea of geometrical similarity. Similarity occurs when one figure is dilated from another figure by a scale factor. In other words, both figures share the same angles but are scaled to be bigger or smaller, causing them to have similar properties. Let's explore this concept further.

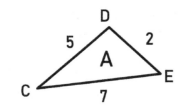

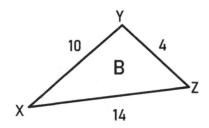

Vocabulary:

<u>Scale factor</u>: a quantity (**k**) multiplying the length of a side to increase or decrease the polygon's size

<u>Reduction</u>: when $0 < k < 1$, causing the polygon to shrink (ex. XZ → CE)

<u>Enlargement</u>: when $k > 1$, causing the polygon to become bigger (ex. DE → YZ)

In the above diagram, we notice 2 triangles A and B. Each side of triangle B has twice the length of the corresponding sides of triangle A. This is because 2 is the scale factor, or the amount multiplied to dilate triangle A.

 ## Proportionality

<u>Proportion</u>: ratios created between corresponding sides of 2 similar triangles are equivalent to one another.

Corresponding sides of similar triangles are **proportional** to one another. In the above diagram, this means that each ratio of any side in Triangle A divided by its corresponding side in Triangle B will be equal to one another; these **proportions** are written below. Also, similar triangles do not have congruent sides but always share **congruent angles**.

$$\frac{XY}{CD} = \frac{YZ}{DE} = \frac{XZ}{CE}$$

$$\angle X \cong \angle C$$
$$\angle Y \cong \angle D$$
$$\angle Z \cong \angle E$$

Properties of Similar Triangles Review

- Similar triangles are dilated by a scale factor

- Similar triangles have corresponding sides that are proportional to one another

- Similar triangles have congruent angles

By setting up proportions between corresponding sides of similar triangles, we can find unknown sides of a triangle. Let's see this concept in the example below.

Example

Knowing triangles ABC and JKM are similar in the diagram below, find the value of x.

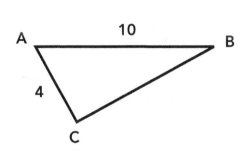

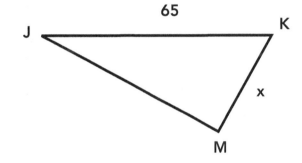

To solve this, we know that both rectangles are similar. Given this, we can create a proportion between corresponding sides JK & AB with KM & CA. Then, substitute the correct lengths for each side and multiply both sides by 4 to isolate and solve for x.

$$\frac{JK}{AB} = \frac{KM}{CA} \longrightarrow \frac{65}{10} = \frac{x}{4} \longrightarrow 4 \cdot \frac{65}{10} = x \longrightarrow x = 26$$

Triangle Similarity Theorems

We can determine if 2 triangles are similar without always needing to know if every corresponding angle is congruent and if every corresponding side is proportional to one another. To do this, we can use the following similarity theorems for triangles.

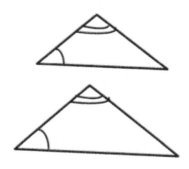

AA Theorem (Angle-Angle Theorem)

If **two angles** of two triangles are **congruent** to each other, then the triangles are said to be **similar**.

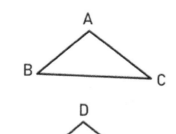

SSS Theorem (Side-Side-Side Theorem)

If **all sides** of two triangles are **proportional** to one other, then the triangles are said to be **similar**.

$$\frac{CA}{ED} = \frac{BC}{FE} = \frac{AB}{DF}$$

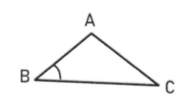

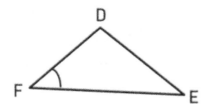

SAS Theorem (Side-Angle-Side Theorem)

If **two sides** of two triangles are **proportional** to each other and their **included** angles are **congruent**, then the triangles are said to be **similar**.

$$\frac{BC}{FE} = \frac{AB}{DF} \qquad \angle B \cong \angle F$$

1.2 Triangle Notation

This lesson will explain the standardized way of labeling triangles without providing a diagram. Take a look at the triangle below.

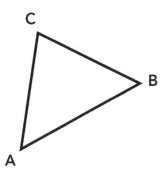

Unless specified in the problem, a triangle is standardized and assumed to be written in the form $\triangle ABC$ where each of the vertices are labeled as A, B, and C. Remember that vertices are <u>always labeled with capital letters</u>.

Additionally, angles do not have to be written in the form of three letters and an angle symbol (ex. $\angle BAC$). Instead, the angle can be simply represented by the letter of the "middle" vertex (ex. $\angle BAC$ can be represented as **A**).

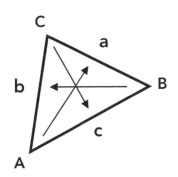

In addition, sides are always represented as lowercase letters. The letter representing the side corresponds to the vertex **opposite** to the side, as shown with the arrows in the diagram. Side BC is represented by letter **a** corresponding to the vertex A.

 Example   **Sketch a triangle with A=50°, B=72°, a=36.**

In this example, the letter of the third vertex is not given. Whenever all the angles or all the sides are not specified in the problem, we assume that the triangle will contain all three angles A, B, and C to form $\triangle ABC$.

To solve the problem, sketch an arbitrary triangle with vertices A, B, C (this is a sketch, so measurements <u>do not need to be scaled</u>). <u>The orientation of the triangle and the order vertices does **not** matter and will not affect the actual triangle measurements.</u> Therefore, any of the triangles shown on the next page would be acceptable.

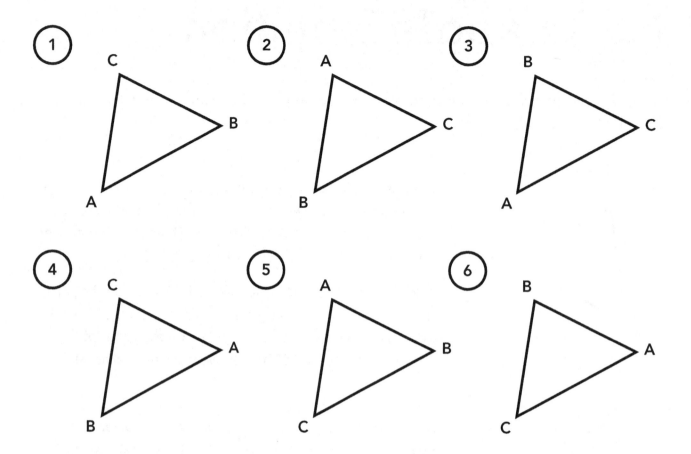

Fill the triangle with the information provided in the problem for respective angles and side measurements to form the triangle. That's it!

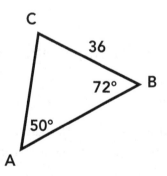

<u>Note:</u> The first sketch of the triangle is used in the above example, but we can use any other variations of the triangles shown above and apply the same concept.

1.1 & 1.2 Practice Problems

For #1-6, determine if triangle ABC is similar to triangle DEF. If so, state the corresponding similarity theorem used.

1 A=54°, B=36°, D=54°, F=94°

2 F=75°, B=75°, e=3, f=6, b=4, c=2

3 E=24°, A=110°, B=46°, d=15, f=9, a=39, b=65

4 A=106.6°, E=25.2°, e=28, f=63, d=49, a=9, b=4, c=7

5 A=100°, B=22°, D=22°, E=58°

6 a=8, f=12, e=15, b=10, d=14, c=7

For #7-10, knowing XYZ ~ CDE, find the missing side prompted below.

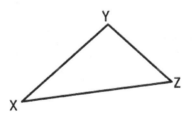
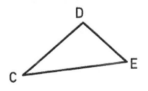

7 x=10, z=9, c=18. Find e.

8 y=25, d=100, c=256. Find x.

9 x=7, y=3, z=6, c=98, e=84. Find d.

10 x=13, d=5, c=27. Find y.

This lesson will introduce different properties and theorems used to describe triangles that will also be useful when learning critical trigonometric concepts later in this book.

 ## Triangle Inequalities

Triangle Inequality Theorem

In a triangle, the sum of any two sides must always be greater than the third side.

$$a + b > c \qquad b + c > a \qquad a + c > b$$

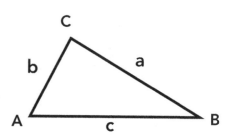

The sum of the longest side and any other side of a triangle will <u>always</u> be greater than the other short side (ex. **b + c > a** and **a + c > b** considering c is the longest side). Therefore, this theorem can be simplified to check if the sum of the two shorter sides (**a + b**) is greater than the longest side (**c**) then it would be a triangle.

Corollary of Triangle Inequality Theorem

In a triangle, the sum of the two shortest sides must be greater than the longest side.

$$a + b > c$$

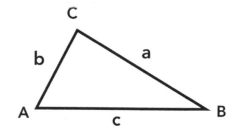

 ## Example 1

Will line segments with lengths a=7, b=10, c=25 form a triangle?

In this problem, we must apply the Corollary of the Triangle Inequality Theorem.
First, identify the two smallest sides (**a** and **b**). Then, calculate the sum of these two sides (7+10 = 17) and compare it to the longest side **c**.
Since 17 < 25, a triangle cannot be formed.

In addition to the inequality theorems on the previous page, Pythagorean inequalities listed below use side lengths to determine the classification of a triangle based on angle.

Pythagorean Inequalities

In a triangle where **c** is the longest side and **a** & **b** are other two short sides of the triangle:

- If $c^2 < a^2 + b^2$, then the triangle is classified as **acute**.
- If $c^2 = a^2 + b^2$, then Pythagorean theorem is applied and the triangle is classified as **right**.
- If $c^2 > a^2 + b^2$, then the triangle is classified as **obtuse**.

 Example 2   **Classify a triangle with sides 17, 19, 5 based on angle.**

Firstly, assign each side to the correct variable based on length: a=5, b=17, c=19 assuming c is the longest side of the triangle.

Second, setup the following expressions above and determine the inequality/equality by substituting the above values and solving for both sides.

$$c^2 \bigcirc a^2 + b^2$$

$$19^2 \bigcirc 17^2 + 5^2$$

$$361 > 314$$

In this example, $c^2 > a^2 + b^2$.
This inequality indicates that the triangle is **obtuse**.

9

Ordering Angles & Sides

While ordering the measurements of angles and sides from the least to the greatest, the following rules can be used:

- The side opposite to the **largest** angle is the **longest** side.
- The side opposite to the **smallest** angle is the **shortest** side.
- The angle opposite to the **longest** side is the **largest** angle.
- The angle opposite to the **shortest** side is the **smallest** angle.

 Example 3   **Order the sides in an ascending order if A=56° & B=82°**

Begin by drawing a sketch of a triangle with the given information. This problem only provides information for angles A & B, so angle C needs to be calculated using the Triangle Sum Theorem: 180° - (56° +82°) = 42°.

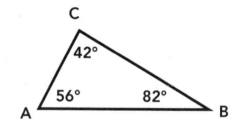

In this example, angle B is the largest angle. This means that the side **b** opposite of angle B, is the longest side.

Since C is the smallest angle, the side **c** opposite of angle C is the shortest side. That means that the length of side **a** is in between **c** and **b**. The following inequality can be written:

$$c < a < b$$

1.3 Practice Problems

For #1-6, identify if the following segment lengths form a triangle.
If so, classify the triangle based on angle.

1 7, 4, 6

2 3, 26, 11

3 12, 3.5, 12.5

4 1, 2, 3

5 6, 9, 12

6 8, 15, 8

For #7-10, order the sides and angles in an ascending order for triangle XYZ.
However, label line segments with two letters (ex. $\overline{XY}$).

7 X=50°, Y=70°

8 z=8, y=19, x=13

9 Z=35°, Y=45°

10 x=26, y=19, z=35

11

Unit 2

Right Triangle Trigonometry

2.1 Special Triangles

In this unit, we will dive into the basics of trigonometry for right triangles. In the last unit, we compared the ratios of sides of similar triangles and, in this lesson, we will introduce what makes 45-45-90 & 30-60-90 triangles so special.

⚙ 45-45-90 Triangle

A 45-45-90 triangle is any right triangle with two 45° acute angles. Since this is the only type of right triangle with two equivalent acute angles, this means their opposite sides will be equivalent to one another as per the **Converse of the Base Angle Theorem**. Thus, these triangles are also known as **isosceles right triangles**. In this diagram, let's label these equivalent sides as **x**.

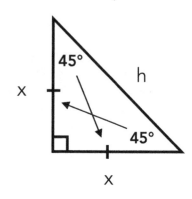

We will use Pythagorean theorem on this triangle to find the hypotenuse in terms of **x** and identify a pattern!

$$h^2 = x^2 + x^2 \longrightarrow h^2 = 2x^2 \longrightarrow h = \sqrt{2x^2} \longrightarrow h = x\sqrt{2}$$

| Pythagorean Theorem | Combine Like Terms | Square root of both sides | Simplify radical |

What can we conclude?

In any 45-45-90 triangle:

The legs of the triangle are <u>equivalent</u> and the <u>hypotenuse is always the length of the leg multiplied by $\sqrt{2}$</u>.

45-45-90 Triangle

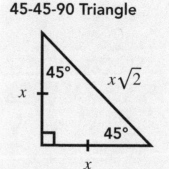

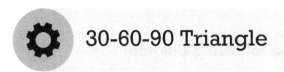 **30-60-90 Triangle**

A 30-60–90 triangle is any right triangle with a 30° and 60° acute angles. In order to identify the ratios of this triangle, let's start off with drawing an arbitrary equilateral triangle below, with each side measuring 2x.

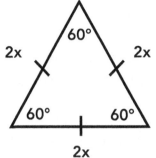

All equilateral triangles are equiangular, so the measure of each angle will be 60°. We can then divide this triangle in half by bisecting the 60° angle to create a 30-60-90 triangle shown below. To solve for the missing height "h", let's use the Pythagorean Theorem.

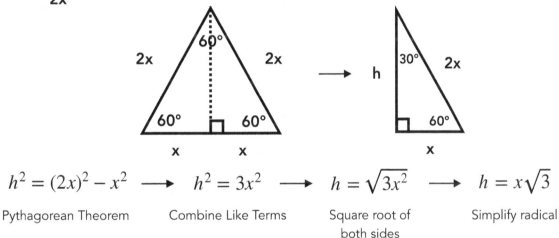

$$h^2 = (2x)^2 - x^2 \longrightarrow h^2 = 3x^2 \longrightarrow h = \sqrt{3x^2} \longrightarrow h = x\sqrt{3}$$

Pythagorean Theorem   Combine Like Terms   Square root of   Simplify radical
                                                            both sides

What can we conclude?

In any 30-60–90 triangle:
The <u>hypotenuse is double the length of the short leg across from 30°</u>.
The <u>long leg across from 60° is the length of the short leg multiplied by $\sqrt{3}$</u>.

30-60-90 Triangle

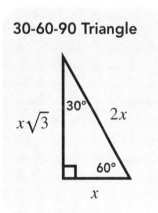

Example 1   **Find x & y in the following diagram.**

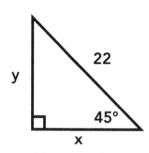

Even though the second 45° angle is not shown here, the Triangle Sum Theorem makes it evident that the above triangle is a 45-45-90 triangle. This means that the triangle is also isosceles, so **x** and **y** are <u>equivalent</u>.

To find **x**, we know that the length of the leg multiplied by $\sqrt{2}$ is equivalent to the length of the hypotenuse. Therefore, we can setup the following equation below and isolate for **x**. Length of **y** would be equal to **x** since both the legs are equivalent.

$$x\sqrt{2} = 22 \longrightarrow x = \frac{22}{\sqrt{2}}\left(\frac{\sqrt{2}}{\sqrt{2}}\right) \longrightarrow x = \frac{22\sqrt{2}}{2} \longrightarrow x = 11\sqrt{2}$$

45-45-90
hypotenuse & leg

Divide by $\sqrt{2}$ on both
sides & rationalize

Rationalize
denominator

Simplify

$$y = x \longrightarrow y = 11\sqrt{2}$$

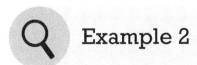 **Example 2**   **Find x & y in the following diagram.**

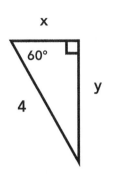

Based on the diagram and using the Triangle Sum Theorem, we can assume the other acute angle is 30°.

This means **x** is the <u>short leg</u> and **y** is the <u>long leg</u>.

The hypotenuse is double the length of the short leg (**x**) as shown in the equation below. We can use this to find **x**.

$$2x = 4 \quad \longrightarrow \quad x = 2$$

30-60–90 hypotenuse   Divide by 2 on
& short leg   both sides

Similarly, **y**, the long leg, would be equal to the length of the short side (**x**) multiplied by $\sqrt{3}$ as shown in the equation below. We can use this formula to find the value of **y**.

$$y = x\sqrt{3} \quad \longrightarrow \quad y = 2\sqrt{3}$$

30-60–90 hypotenuse   Substitute for x
& long leg

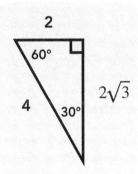

2.1 Practice Problems

Using the triangles below and the information provided in each problem, find all sides of each triangle.

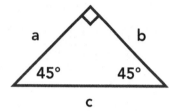

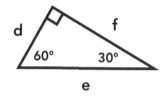

1   a=10, d=7

2   c=15, e=8

3   b=14, f=12

4   d=6, c=10

5   f=6, b=d

6   c=16, e=a

7   e=20, c=f

8   b=9, d=c

2.2 Trigonometric Ratios

In the previous lesson, we explored the relationships between sides of <u>special</u> right triangles. In this lesson, we will use basic trigonometric ratios to describe the relationship between the sides and angles of ANY **right** triangle.

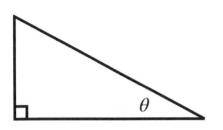

Let's take a look at the right triangle on the left with an acute angle θ called **theta**, a conventional Greek letter used for angles.

From the <u>perspective of an angle θ</u>, there are 3 basic trigonometric ratios for comparing various sides of a triangle:
sine (sin), cosine (cos), and tangent (tan)

Tangent Ratio

Tangent is the <u>ratio</u> of the **OPPOSITE LEG** from θ over the **ADJACENT LEG** near θ

$$\tan \theta = \frac{\text{opposite}}{\text{adjacent}}$$

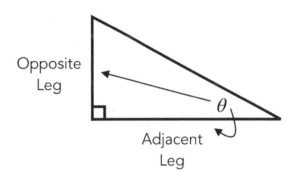

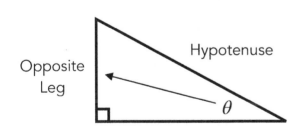

Sine Ratio

Sine is the <u>ratio</u> of the **OPPOSITE LEG** from θ over the triangle's **HYPOTENUSE**

$$\sin \theta = \frac{\text{opposite}}{\text{hypotenuse}}$$

Cosine Ratio

Cosine is the <u>ratio</u> of the **ADJACENT LEG** near θ over the triangle's **HYPOTENUSE**

$$\cos \theta = \frac{\text{adjacent}}{\text{hypotenuse}}$$

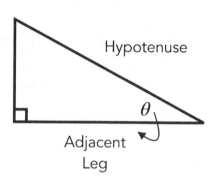

Hypotenuse

θ

Adjacent
Leg

TIP!

To remember the ratios, you can use the acronym **"Soh-Cah-Toa"**.

$$S\frac{O}{H} \quad C\frac{A}{H} \quad T\frac{O}{A}$$

Sine is **o**pposite over **h**ypotenuse, **C**osine is **a**djacent over **h**ypotenuse, and **T**angent is **o**pposite over **a**djacent.

Example

In the following diagram, Find the cosine, sine, and tangent ratios of θ

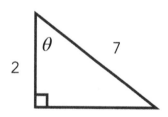

First, we can find the cosine ratio by identifying the **adjacent** leg near θ (2) and dividing it by the **hypotenuse** (7).

$$\cos \theta = \frac{\text{adjacent}}{\text{hypotenuse}} \quad \longrightarrow \quad \cos \theta = \frac{2}{7}$$

To find the sine ratio, we need to divide the **opposite** leg from θ by the **hypotenuse**. However, the above diagram does not provide the length of the opposite side (say **x**), so we need to find it using the Pythagorean Theorem.

$$2^2 + x^2 = 7^2 \longrightarrow x^2 = 45 \longrightarrow x = 3\sqrt{5}$$

Pythagorean Theorem   Subtract 4 from   Square root both sides
                       both sides   & simplify radical

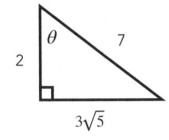

From there, substitute the opposite leg and hypotenuse into the ratio!

$$\sin\theta = \frac{\text{opposite}}{\text{hypotenuse}} \longrightarrow \sin\theta = \frac{3\sqrt{5}}{7}$$

Finally, to find tangent ratio, we need to divide the **opposite** leg from θ ($3\sqrt{5}$) by the **adjacent** leg near θ (2).

$$\tan\theta = \frac{\text{opposite}}{\text{adjacent}} \longrightarrow \tan\theta = \frac{3\sqrt{5}}{2}$$

2.2 Practice Problems

For #1-6, find the indicated ratio of angle A.

1   tan A

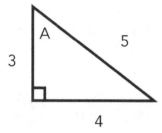

2   cos A

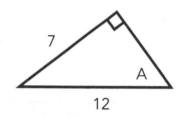

3   2 sin A

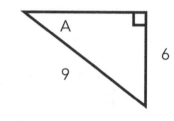

4   cos A

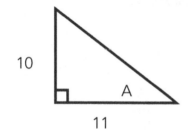

5   If $\sin B = \dfrac{8}{13}$, find tan A

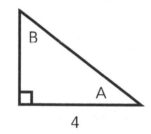

6   5 sin A

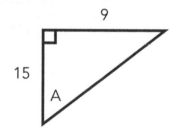

For #7-8, find ALL ratios for angles A and B.

7

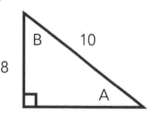

8

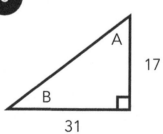

2.3 Solving for Sides

Now that we have understood how to use trigonometric ratios to describe relationships between the sides and angles of any right triangle, in this lesson we will use those ratios to solve for missing sides of a triangle.

 Example 1 **Find x in the triangle below.**

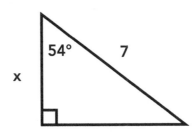

To find the length of missing sides, we would typically use the Pythagorean Theorem or similar proportions, but none of these options can be applied here because we only know one side. However, the side **x** is **adjacent** to the angle measure (54°) and the **hypotenuse** is known (7), so we could setup a **cosine** ratio with respect to 54° as shown below.

$$\cos(54°) = \frac{x}{7}$$

Then, since we want to solve it for the side **x**, we can multiply 7 on both sides to isolate **x**.

$$x = 7\cos(54°)$$

How do we find the cosine ratio of 54°? Well, we can use a scientific calculator! To evaluate any trigonometric ratio on a calculator, follow the steps below:

1. Make sure calculator is in <u>DEG mode</u>
2. Press "SIN", "COS", or "TAN" button (In this example, "COS")
3. Type the angle measurement without any degree sign (In this example, 54)
4. Press "ENTER"

In this problem, we evaluate cos(54°) to be approximately 0.588. We can substitute this value into above equation and multiply accordingly.

$$x = 7\cos(54°) \longrightarrow x \approx 7 \cdot 0.588 \longrightarrow x \approx 4.116$$

TIP! Although you may round the cos(54°) on paper as 0.588, always leave it as the actual decimal value shown on the calculator (0.587785...). This ensures your answer is not significantly off due to rounding errors.

🔍 **Example 2**   **Find b in the triangle below.**

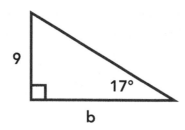

Let's begin solving this problem by trying to find **b**. Since we are given the <u>opposite</u> side from 17° (9) and we need to find the <u>adjacent</u> side **b**, the tangent ratio can be used.

$$\tan(17°) = \frac{9}{b}$$

To isolate for **b**, multiply **b** on both sides and divide by tan(17°) on both sides as well. Then, evaluate tan(17°) in a calculator and simplify the expression accordingly.

$$b \cdot \tan(17°) = 9 \longrightarrow b = \frac{9}{\tan(17°)} \longrightarrow b \approx \frac{9}{0.306} \longrightarrow b \approx 29.41$$

For #1-4, find the missing side 'a'.

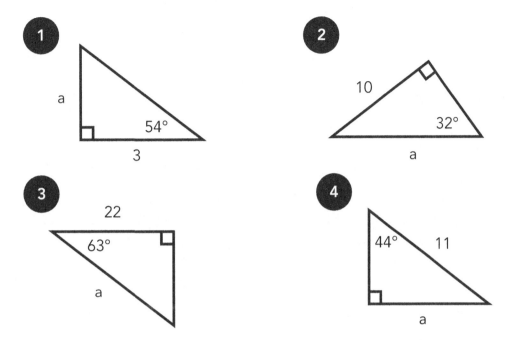

For #7-8, find the unknown variables 'A' and 'b'.

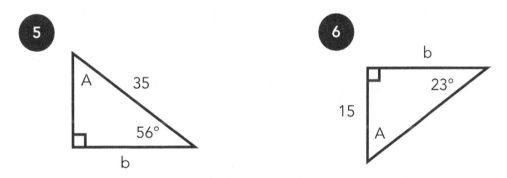

For #7-8, find the missing sides 'a' and 'b'.

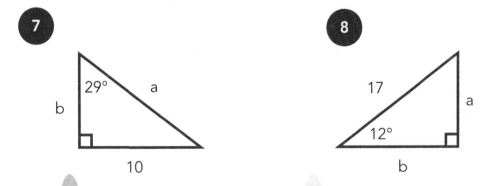

2.4 Inverse Trigonometry

In the previous lesson, we explored how to use trigonometric ratios to find the length of missing <u>sides</u>. In this lesson, we will expand our understanding to learn how to utilize trigonometric ratios to find the measures of unknown <u>angles</u>.

Inverse Ratios

In standard trigonometric ratios, we take the sine, cosine, or tangent of an <u>angle</u> to output its <u>ratio</u>. However, inverse trigonometric ratios perform the opposite operation by taking the sine inverse ($\sin^{-1}$), cosine inverse ($\cos^{-1}$), or tangent inverse ($\tan^{-1}$) of a <u>ratio</u> to find the corresponding <u>angle</u> that produces it.

$$\sin(50°) = 0.766$$
$$\updownarrow$$
$$\sin^{-1}(0.766) = 50°$$

As shown below, here are the definitions of the inverse ratios for sine, cosine, and tangent.

$$\theta = \sin^{-1}\left(\frac{\text{opposite}}{\text{hypotenuse}}\right) \quad \theta = \cos^{-1}\left(\frac{\text{adjacent}}{\text{hypotenuse}}\right) \quad \theta = \tan^{-1}\left(\frac{\text{opposite}}{\text{adjacent}}\right)$$

Inverse Notation

There are two acceptable notations for inverse ratios. First, they can be labeled with a -1 subscript as shown above, and <u>this does **NOT** mean the ratio is raised to the -1 power</u>. It is simply a notation to signify inverse (like $f(x)$ & $f^{-1}(x)$) and does not relate to exponents.

$$\sin^{-1} x \neq (\sin x)^{-1}$$

Second, another way to write an inverse ratio is using the prefix "arc". For example, $\sin^{-1} x$ can also be written as $\arcsin x$, $\cos^{-1} x = \arccos x$, and $\tan^{-1} x = \arctan x$. All of these forms mean the same thing, just different notations.

 **Example**

Find X in the triangle below.

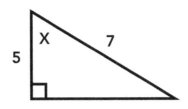

In this problem, we need to find the measure of angle X as shown. Well, we are given the **adjacent** side and **hypotenuse** in the diagram, so a **cosine** ratio can be setup:

$$\cos(X) = \frac{5}{7}$$

To isolate for the angle X, we can perform the inverse cosine operation onto both sides of the equation. As you know that $f^{-1}(f(x)) = x$ for any function, similarly $\cos^{-1}(\cos(x)) = x$ as well. So, the left side of the equation will isolate angle **X** while the right side will be the inverse cosine ratio of 5/7.

$$\cos^{-1}[\cos(X)] = \cos^{-1}\left(\frac{5}{7}\right) \longrightarrow X = \cos^{-1}\left(\frac{5}{7}\right)$$

How do we find the inverse cosine ratio of 54°? Follow the following steps on a scientific calculator:

1. Make sure calculator is in <u>DEG mode</u>
2. Press the "2nd" button (This will perform the INVERSE trigonometric ratio)
3. Press "SIN", "COS", or "TAN" button (In this example, "COS")
4. Type the ratio (In this example, 5/7)
5. Press "ENTER"

In this problem, we evaluate $\cos^{-1}(5/7)$ to be approximately 44.415, and this is our final answer for the measure of angle X.

$$X \approx 44.42°$$

2.4 Practice Problems

For #1-4, find the missing angle A.

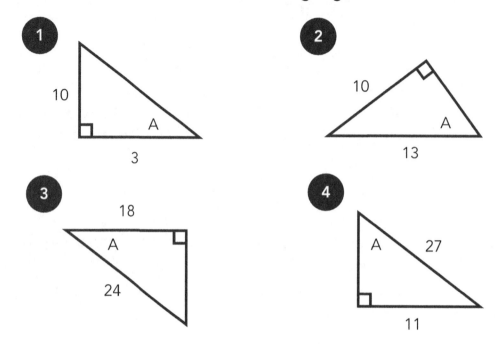

For #5-6, find the unknown angles A & B.

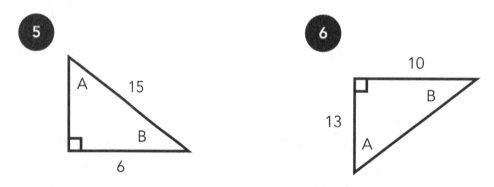

For #7-8, find the missing angle A and the missing side 'b'.

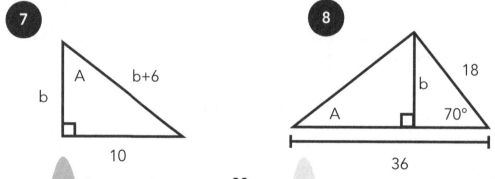

2.5 Reciprocal Ratios

In lessons 2.2 to 2.4, we have learned and applied the 3 basic and fundamental trigonometric ratios: sine, cosine, and tangent. In this lesson, we will explore 3 additional trigonometric **reciprocal** ratios: <u>cosecant</u>, <u>secant</u>, and <u>cotangent</u>.

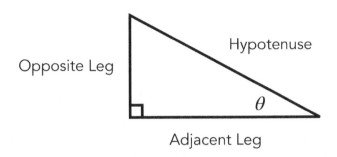

Based on the triangle shown above, listed below are the definitions of the 3 additional trigonometric ratios in terms of the angle θ.

Cosecant Ratio

Cosecant is the <u>ratio</u> of the triangle's **HYPOTENUSE** over the **OPPOSITE LEG** from θ

$$\csc \theta = \frac{\text{hypotenuse}}{\text{opposite}}$$

Secant Ratio

Secant is the <u>ratio</u> of the triangle's **HYPOTENUSE** over the **ADJACENT LEG** near θ

$$\sec \theta = \frac{\text{hypotenuse}}{\text{adjacent}}$$

Cotangent Ratio

Cotangent is the <u>ratio</u> of the **ADJACENT LEG** from θ over the **OPPOSITE LEG** near θ

$$\cot \theta = \frac{\text{adjacent}}{\text{opposite}}$$

Although these definitions of csc, sec, and cot are correct, they are usually expressed in a different way. Let's place these side-by-side with the previous trigonometric ratios we learned (sine, cosine, tangent) and find a pattern.

$$\csc \theta = \frac{\text{hypotenuse}}{\text{opposite}} \longleftrightarrow \sin \theta = \frac{\text{opposite}}{\text{hypotenuse}}$$

$$\sec \theta = \frac{\text{hypotenuse}}{\text{adjacent}} \longleftrightarrow \cos \theta = \frac{\text{adjacent}}{\text{hypotenuse}}$$

$$\cot \theta = \frac{\text{adjacent}}{\text{opposite}} \longleftrightarrow \tan \theta = \frac{\text{opposite}}{\text{adjacent}}$$

Notice how each of these paired ratios have their denominators and numerators flipped! This means they are **reciprocals** of one another, or written in the form of $\dfrac{1}{\text{ratio}}$.

Thus, **csc, sec,** and **cot** are known as the <u>**reciprocal ratios**</u>. Reciprocal ratio definitions are usually written in this form:

Reciprocal Ratios

$$\csc \theta = \frac{1}{\sin \theta} \qquad \sec \theta = \frac{1}{\cos \theta} \qquad \cot \theta = \frac{1}{\tan \theta}$$

NOTE

It is easy to confuse **cosecant** to be the opposite of the cosine ratio since they both start with "co", but it is actually the opposite of **sine**. Same applies for **secant** and **cosine**.

Also, if you want to evaluate the cosecant, secant, or cotangent of any angle using a calculator, there is typically no direct function for this. Instead, you will need to utilize the above definition of reciprocal ratios by using the sin, cos, or tan operations. For example, $\cot(42°)$ can be rewritten as $1/\tan(42°)$ or $[\tan(42°)]^{-1}$ in a calculator.

Q Example $\quad$ If $\csc\theta = \dfrac{7}{5}$, find the remaining trigonometric ratios.

To find the other trigonometric ratios, we will need to setup a triangle diagram. To know the length of the legs and hypotenuse, we can use the ratio given above. **Cosecant** is the ratio of the hypotenuse over the opposite side, so we can treat **7** as the hypotenuse and **5** as the opposite side.

$$\csc\theta = \frac{7}{5} \longleftarrow \frac{\text{hypotenuse}}{\text{opposite}}$$

Using this, we can draw the following triangle below. Then, we can use Pythagorean Theorem to solve for the missing adjacent side and formulate the remaining ratios.

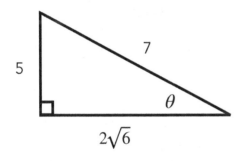

$$\sqrt{7^2 - 5^2} = \sqrt{24} = 2\sqrt{6}$$

Hypotenuse: 7
Opposite Leg: 5
Adjacent Leg: $2\sqrt{6}$

$$\sin\theta = \frac{5}{7} \qquad\qquad \csc\theta = \frac{7}{5}$$

$$\cos\theta = \frac{2\sqrt{6}}{7} \qquad\qquad \sec\theta = \frac{7}{2\sqrt{6}} \longrightarrow \frac{7\sqrt{6}}{12}$$

$$\tan\theta = \frac{5}{2\sqrt{6}} \longrightarrow \frac{5\sqrt{6}}{12} \qquad \cot\theta = \frac{2\sqrt{6}}{5}$$

2.5 Practice Problems

Use the given ratio provided in the problem to find the missing ratio without using inverse trigonometry.

(Hint: In a ratio, treat variables in the same manner as numerical values for #7-9)

1 $\csc x = \dfrac{9}{4}$

Find $\sin x$

2 $\cos x = \dfrac{5}{3}$

Find $\tan x$

3 $\sec x = \dfrac{11}{7}$

Find $\cot x$

4 $\cot x = 8.75$

Find $\cos x$

5 $\sec x = \dfrac{26}{15}$

Find $\sin x$

6 $\sin x = \dfrac{5\sqrt{5}}{12}$

Find $\cos x$

7 $\cot x = \dfrac{3}{a}$

Find $\sec x$

8 $\cos x = \dfrac{\sqrt{b}}{8}$

Find $\sin x$

9 $\csc x = 0.65c$

Find $\tan x$

2.6 Special Ratios

In lesson 2.1, we were introduced to the special angles 30°, 45°, & 60° angles and learned how to find missing sides of 45-45-90 and 30-60-90 triangles. In this lesson, we will learn how to find the trigonometric ratios of these special angles without having to use a calculator.

Since similar triangles share the same trigonometric ratios, we can take the triangles from lesson 2.1 and divide by **x** from all sides to illustrate the ratios numerically. This is shown below.

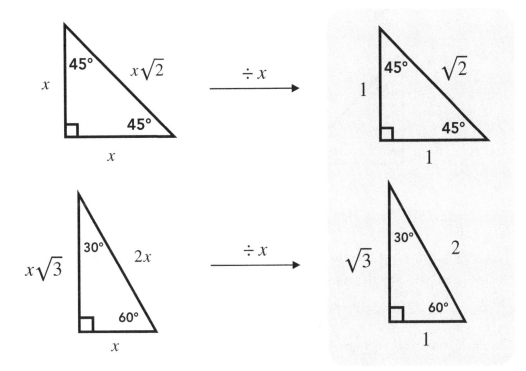

Using the simplified triangles above, we can create the following trigonometric ratios below. NOTE: It is important to be **familiar** with the value of ratios for cosine, sine, and tangent, but it is not necessary to memorize them as it can be easily driven as shown below.

$$\sin 45° = \frac{1}{\sqrt{2}} = \frac{\sqrt{2}}{2} \qquad \sin 30° = \frac{1}{2} \qquad \sin 60° = \frac{\sqrt{3}}{2}$$

$$\cos 45° = \frac{1}{\sqrt{2}} = \frac{\sqrt{2}}{2} \qquad \cos 30° = \frac{\sqrt{3}}{2} \qquad \cos 60° = \frac{1}{2}$$

$$\tan 45° = \frac{\sqrt{2}}{\sqrt{2}} = 1 \qquad \tan 30° = \frac{1}{\sqrt{3}} = \frac{\sqrt{3}}{3} \qquad \tan 30° = \frac{\sqrt{3}}{1} = \sqrt{3}$$

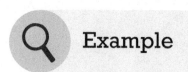 **Example**   **Find** $\sin 45°$

To start, it is recommended to redraw a simplified 45-45-90 triangle. From there, pick one of the 45° angles in the triangle and divide the opposite leg by the hypotenuse.

The result should be $\dfrac{1}{\sqrt{2}}$, and by rationalizing the denominator, the final result is $\dfrac{\sqrt{2}}{2}$.

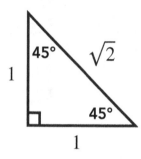

$$\sin 45° = \frac{1}{\sqrt{2}} = \frac{\sqrt{2}}{2}$$

TIP

To easily remember the ratios, always note that for 45° angles, cosine and sine are the same ($\sqrt{2}\,/\,2$) and since both legs are equivalent, the tangent is 1.

Similarly, the sine and cosine for 30° and 60° are interchangeably 1/2 or $\sqrt{3}\,/\,2$.

2.6 Practice Problems

Fill in the triangles below and for #1-9, evaluate the ratios.

45-45-90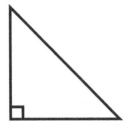

30-60-90

1 $\sin 30°$

2 $\cos 60°$

3 $\tan 45°$

4 $\cot 60°$

5 $\csc 45°$

6 $\sec 30°$

7 $\cos 45°$

8 $\cot 30°$

9 $\csc 60°$

Are you ready to apply all of your right triangle trigonometry learning so far to some real world problems? In these problems, we will often come across the terms "angle of elevation" and "angle of depression", so let's learn what they mean using this diagram below.

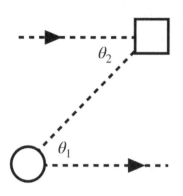

Vocabulary:

Horizontal: A straight line traveling on a plane, also known as the **line of sight**.

Angle of Elevation (θ_1): The angle formed between the horizontal of one object ◯ and an object **above** it ☐.

Angle of Depression (θ_2): The angle formed between the horizontal of one object ☐ and an object **below** it ◯.

Since horizontals are <u>parallel</u> to one another, the Alternate Interior Angles Theorem can be applied. It states that angle θ_1 must be congruent to angle θ_2. This means <u>the angle of depression will always have the same measure as the angle of elevation</u>.

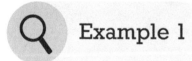 **Example 1**

Michael stands 15 ft away from a tree. The angle of elevation from his line of sight to the top of the tree is 46°. Michael is 5ft tall. Find the height of the tree.

To begin, we must always draw a diagram of the situation described. Michael and the tree stand on the same ground, and we know that his height is 5ft but the height of the tree is unknown. Additionally, the angle of elevation from his **eye** to the top of the tree is 46° located 15 ft away from the tree. The length of this embedded triangle can be described as an arbitrary variable **x**.

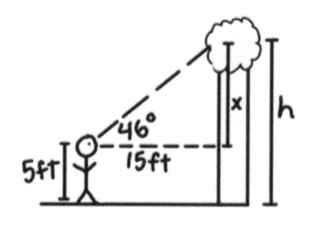

Once again, the goal of this problem is to find **h,** the height of the tree. As per the diagram, since $h = x + 5$, we need to begin by finding **x**. To do so, we can set up a tangent ratio of the inside triangle as shown below.

$$\tan 46° = \frac{x}{15}$$

$$\downarrow$$

$$x = 15 \tan 46°$$

Before we evaluate $15 \tan 46°$ on our calculator, substitute **x** into the equation $h = x + 5$ to solve for the final height.

$$h = x + 5 \quad \longrightarrow \quad h = 15 \tan 46° + 5 \quad \longrightarrow \quad h \approx 15.53 + 5 \approx 20.53 \text{ ft}$$

Q **Example 2**

A ladder lies diagonally on a fence at a 37° angle and the horizontal distance from the bottom of the ladder to the fence is 5 ft longer than the height of the fence. How long is the ladder?

Once again, we must begin with a diagram. A ladder is laying diagonally on a vertical fence at 37°, so the angle of elevation is 37° and the ladder is the **hypotenuse** of this triangle (labeled as **x**). The vertical fence is a leg labeled **h** and the horizontal leg is 5ft longer than the height, so it is labeled as **h + 5**.

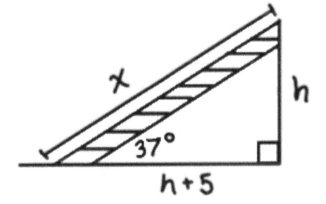

To solve this problem, we must create a system of two equations involving the variable **x**. To do so, we can begin by creating the sine ratio for 37° and isolate for **h** as shown.

$$\sin 37° = \frac{h}{x} \longrightarrow h = x \sin 37°$$

Sine ratio   Multiply by x on both sides

For the second equation, we can take the cosine ratio of 37° and <u>substitute</u> **h** for the expression created above: $x \sin 37°$. Then, isolate for **x** and evaluate the expression.

$$\cos 37° = \frac{h + 5}{x} \longrightarrow \cos 37° = \frac{x \sin 37° + 5}{x}$$

Cosine ratio   Substitute for h

$$\longrightarrow x \cos 37° = x \sin 37° + 5 \longrightarrow x(\cos 37° - \sin 37°) = 5$$

Multiply by x on both sides   Subtract $x \sin 37°$ from
both sides and factor x

$$\longrightarrow x = \frac{5}{\cos 37° - \sin 37°} \longrightarrow x \approx 25.4 \text{ ft}$$

Divide by $(\cos 37° - \sin 37°)$
from both sides

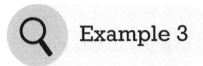

Example 3

In front of a lighthouse on shore, there are two boats at sea. Boat A makes an angle of depression of 20° with the top of the lighthouse, and Boat B being much further makes an angle of depression of 12°. If Boat B is 13 mi from Boat A, how far is Boat A from the lighthouse?

For this diagram, we need to illustrate a tall lighthouse with Boat A and Boat B lying on the sea. Boat A has a greater angle of depression, so it will be closer to the shore than Boat B. From the top of the lighthouse to Boat A is an angle of 20° and to Boat B is 12°. However, since angle of depression is equivalent to elevation, we can illustrate the 20° and 12° as angles of elevation to visualize the triangles easily. The distance from Boat A to shore is **x** and the height of the lighthouse is **h**.

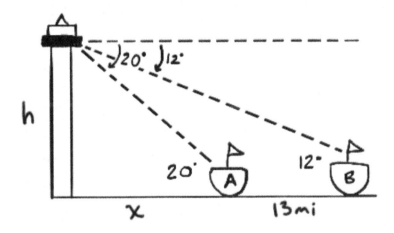

Below is a simplified version of the diagram to illustrate the two embedded triangles:

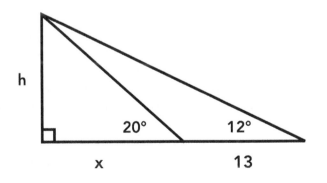

Our goal is to find **x**. To do so, we need to create two tangent ratios: one for the 20° angle and one for the 12° angle.

Note that for tan 12°, the adjacent leg is the base of the **larger** triangle: x + 13.

$$\tan 20° = \frac{h}{x} \qquad \tan 12° = \frac{h}{x + 13}$$

In both equations, let's isolate for **h**. This way, we can perform a system of equations to solve for **x** as shown below.

$$h = x \tan 20°$$

Multiply by **x** on
both sides

$$h = (\tan 12°)(x + 13)$$

Multiply by **x+3**
on both sides

$$x \tan 20° = (\tan 12°)(x + 13) \longrightarrow x \tan 20° = x \tan 12° + 13 \tan 12°$$

System of equations

Distributive Property

$$\longrightarrow x(\tan 20° - \tan 12°) = 13 \tan 12° \longrightarrow x = \frac{13}{\tan 20° - \tan 12°}$$

Subtract $x \tan 12°$ from
both sides and factor x

Divide by $(\tan 20° - \tan 12°)$
from both sides

$$x \approx 85.86 \text{ mi}$$

2.7 Practice Problems

Solve the following word problems below.

1 Josh is 5.2 ft tall and stands 6 ft in front of a 13.2 ft flagpole. What is the angle of elevation from the tip of his shadow to the top of the flagpole?

2 An anchor attached to a rope is thrown 45 ft below sea level at an angle of depression of 30° from the ship. How long is the rope?

3 A flying plane creates an angle of depression of 7° with your house. Then, after flying for some time, the plane is 20 mi away from your house and creates an angle of depression of 16°. How far did it travel?

4 Gabriella skies down a mountain slope of 30° in 29 sec. Thomas skies on the other side of the mountain at a slope of 60° in 14.7 sec. If the mountain is 936m tall, who is faster and by how much (m/s)?
NOTE: speed = distance/time

5 Sam & Kaitlyn are playing basketball. Sam, playing defense, creates an angle of elevation of 48° with the top of the hoop. Kaitlyn, who has the ball, stands 6 ft ahead of him, making an angle of elevation of 26° with the top of the hoop. How tall is the basketball hoop?

6 The door of an A-frame tent is an isosceles triangle. The angles formed by the tent door to the ground (the base angles) are 74° and the height of the tent is 10 ft. Calculate the perimeter of the tent door.

Unit

3

Unit Circle Trigonometry

3.1 Radians

Welcome to a new unit! In this unit, we will explore how to broaden our scope of trigonometry and apply it to the coordinate plane. This lesson will introduce a new standardized unit for angle measurement called radians instead of degrees.

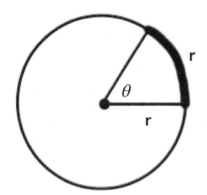

One radian (rad), shown as θ, is described as the central angle that creates an <u>arc length equivalent to the length of the radius</u>. Even though the length of a radius varies from circle to circle, the <u>measure of a radian</u> will <u>always remain constant</u>. The diagram to the left shows theta measuring one radian, which is always 57 degrees.

How many radians does it take to cover **one full rotation of a circle (360°)?**
The circumference of a circle is $2\pi r$, meaning the length of the circumference is 2π radii. Since 1 radian covers 1 radius, this means 2π radii are covered by 2π radians.

Since <u>2π radians and 360° both measure one full rotation</u> in a circle, both values are equivalent to one another!

$$360° = 2\pi \text{ rad}$$

$$360° = 2\pi \text{ rad} \xrightarrow{\div 2} 180° = \pi \text{ rad}$$

This simplifies the conversion between radians and degrees since π rad is the same as 180°. For special angles previously described in Unit 2 (30°, 45°, 60° and 90°), the radian measure can be simply found by dividing $180° = \pi$ rad by a common factor (such as 6, 4, 3, 2) as shown below:

$$360° = 2\pi \text{ rad} \qquad 180° = \pi \text{ rad} \qquad 90° = \frac{\pi}{2} \text{ rad}$$

$$30° = \frac{\pi}{6} \text{ rad} \qquad 60° = \frac{\pi}{3} \text{ rad} \qquad 45° = \frac{\pi}{4} \text{ rad}$$

The following proportions can be used to convert between radians and degrees by substituting for either x or y:

$$\frac{\pi \text{ rad}}{180°} = \frac{x \text{ rad}}{y°} \qquad \longleftrightarrow \qquad \frac{180°}{\pi \text{ rad}} = \frac{y°}{x \text{ rad}}$$

Degrees to radians   Radians to degrees

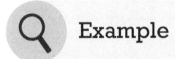 **Example**

Convert the following to either radians or degrees:

a) 72°   b) 6π rad   c) 135°

For each of the problems (a, b, c), simply substitute for y or x in the proportions described above: $\frac{\pi \text{ rad}}{180°} = \frac{x \text{ rad}}{y°}$ or $\frac{180°}{\pi \text{ rad}} = \frac{y°}{x \text{ rad}}$. For problems **a** and **c**, it is preferred to use the first proportion and for problem **b**, it is preferred to use the second proportion. However, <u>either proportion would work.</u>

$$a) \ \frac{\pi \text{ rad}}{180°} = \frac{\theta \text{ rad}}{72°} \rightarrow \theta = \frac{72° \cdot \pi \text{ rad}}{180°} \rightarrow \theta = \frac{2\pi}{5} \text{ rad}$$

$$b) \ \frac{180°}{\pi \text{ rad}} = \frac{\theta°}{6\pi \text{ rad}} \rightarrow \theta = \frac{180° \cdot 6\pi \text{ rad}}{\pi \text{ rad}} \rightarrow \theta = 1080°$$

$$c) \ \frac{\pi \text{ rad}}{180°} = \frac{\theta \text{ rad}}{135°} \rightarrow \theta = \frac{135° \cdot \pi \text{ rad}}{180°} \rightarrow \theta = \frac{3\pi}{4} \text{ rad}$$

NOTE

Degrees must always use the (°) symbol but radians <u>may or may not</u> be written with **rad**.

3.1 Practice Problems

Convert each of the following angles to either degrees or radians.

1 $84°$ **2** $\dfrac{4\pi}{9}$ **3** $459°$

4 $\dfrac{17\pi}{8}$ **5** $\dfrac{11\pi}{6}$ **6** $150°$

7 $300°$ **8** $\dfrac{2\pi}{3}$ **9** $\dfrac{5\pi}{4}$

In this lesson, we will transition to the coordinate plane to explore the trigonometry of triangles and angles in more detail. Let's understand some new vocabulary regarding angles!

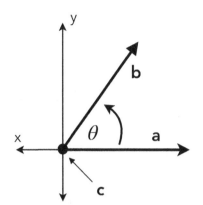

Initial side (a): a ray extending from the vertex onto the x-axis

Terminal side (b): a ray extending from the vertex to create the angle θ with the initial side

Standard position: Angle's vertex is located on (0,0)

Angles are located in standard position unless otherwise specified. The initial side is always placed on the x-axis and the terminal side is mobile and can change orientation. Typically, we have defined angles to not have a negative measurement and cannot measure over 360°. However, these rules do not apply on the coordinate plane.

(a) If the terminal side of an angle moves in a **counter-clockwise** direction, the angle measure is **positive**.

(b) Therefore, when the terminal side moves **clockwise**, the angle measure is **negative**.

(c) Once angles rotate 360° (2π) in the positive direction, the angle can continue to cross the initial side and repeat a new rotation, making the angle measure **greater than 360°**.

a)   b)   c)

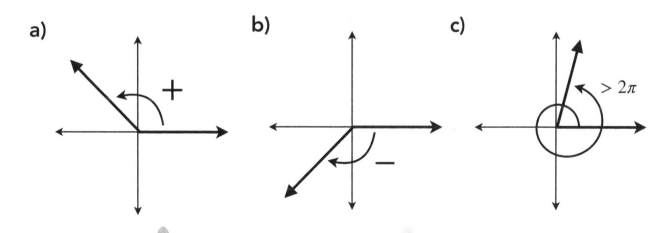

Sometimes, it is difficult to visualize angles such as 1050° or -475° on the coordinate plane since we are so used to looking at angles $0° < \theta < 360°$. **Coterminal angles** can facilitate this process and make angles easier to visualize.

Coterminal angles: Different angles that share the <u>same terminal side</u>

For instance, the angle 225° can be illustrated using its negative coterminal angle -135° or its positive coterminal angle 585°. Coterminal angles are found by <u>adding or subtracting 360° (2π) from an angle measurement</u>, which increases or decreases the angle measure by a rotation.

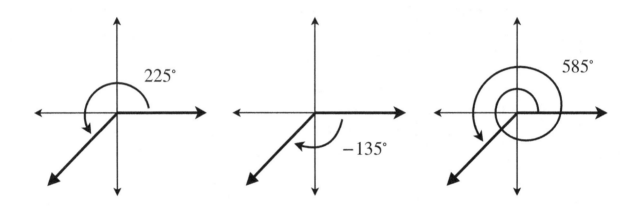

Q **Example 1**   Identify a positive and negative coterminal angle for $\frac{\pi}{6}$

To find the positive coterminal angle, complete one rotation in the counter-clockwise direction by adding 2π.

$$\frac{\pi}{6} + 2\pi \longrightarrow \frac{\pi}{6} + \frac{12\pi}{6} \longrightarrow \frac{13\pi}{6}$$

To find the negative coterminal angle, complete one rotation in the clockwise direction by subtracting 2π.

$$\frac{\pi}{6} - 2\pi \longrightarrow \frac{\pi}{6} - \frac{12\pi}{6} \longrightarrow -\frac{11\pi}{6}$$

In the next example, we will assimilate how to graph radians on the coordinate plane without needing to convert to degrees.

🔍 **Example 2**   Graph $-\dfrac{3\pi}{4}$

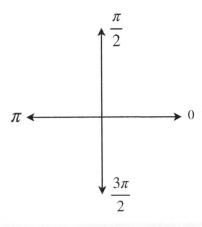

First, label each axis with the corresponding positive angle from the initial side.

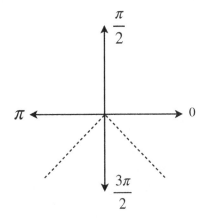

The denominator of the radian fraction is 4, so divide π into 4 equal pieces as shown (in the negative direction).

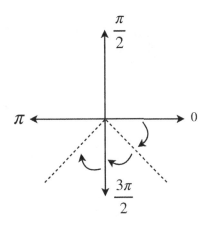

The angle $-\dfrac{3\pi}{4}$ can be rewritten as $3 \cdot \dfrac{-\pi}{4}$, meaning the terminal sides turns $-\dfrac{\pi}{4}$ three times.

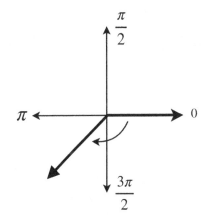

On the dashed line located in Quadrant 3, draw the terminal side with a small directional arrow indicating if the angle is positive or negative.

49

3.2 Practice Problems

For #1-5, identify a positive and negative coterminal angle for each angle.

1 $237°$

2 $-236°$

3 $-\dfrac{9\pi}{2}$

4 $\dfrac{17\pi}{8}$

5 $\dfrac{16\pi}{3}$

For #6-8, sketch the following radian angle on the given coordinate plane.

Note: The dotted lines on graphs for #6-8 are guides.
For instance, the first quadrant guides are to help outline the angles $\dfrac{\pi}{6}, \dfrac{\pi}{4}, \dfrac{\pi}{3}$.

6 $\dfrac{5\pi}{4}$

7 $\dfrac{11\pi}{6}$

8 $\dfrac{8\pi}{3}$

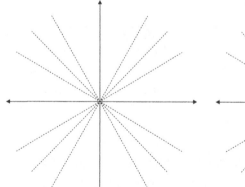

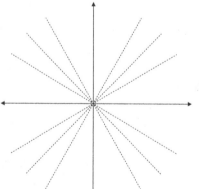

3.3 Unit Circle

Welcome to this lesson about the unit circle! Here we will learn to apply trigonometry on the angles plotted on the coordinate plane from the previous lesson. What is the unit circle though?

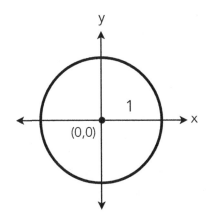

Unit Circle: A circle by the equation $x^2 + y^2 = 1$ with its center at the origin (0,0) and a radius of 1.

To begin with, let's focus on just the first quadrant of the unit circle. We will try to embed a right triangle in the unit circle as shown below, intersecting at some point (x,y). The horizontal distance from (0,0) to (x,0) is **x**, and the vertical distance from (x,y) to (x,0) is **y**. This triangle has an arbitrary angle θ and the hypotenuse is the length of the radius, so it is **1**.

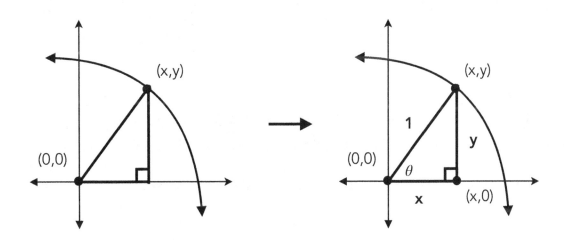

For a moment, let's isolate the triangle from the coordinate plane. Since we know right triangle trigonometry, let's try to find trigonometric ratios of θ, specifically sine and cosine. Think about why this is special.

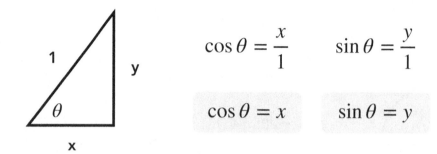

$$\cos \theta = \frac{x}{1} \qquad \sin \theta = \frac{y}{1}$$

$$\cos \theta = x \qquad \sin \theta = y$$

If $\cos \theta = x$, then Transitive Property of Equality states $x = \cos \theta$, same for $y = \sin \theta$. This means that all **x** values in the previous diagram can be replaced with the expression $\cos \theta$, and all **y** values can be replaced with $\sin \theta$.

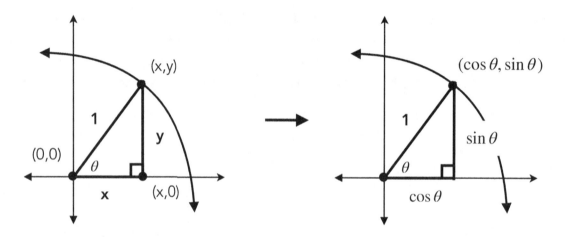

This means that any point and any angle on the unit circle can be written in terms of sine and cosine of the center angle formed from the terminal side. This is how the unit circle provides us a visual representation of trigonometric ratios.

X always represents the cosine ratio, Y always represents the sine ratio

The diagram shown above only illustrates this concept in the first quadrant, but it extends into the other quadrants as well. Although creating a right triangle with an initial side lying on the positive x-axis is not possible in quadrants 2, 3, & 4, we can still find the sine or cosine of θ using the intersected coordinates.

For example, the terminal side of the angle 106° intersects with the unit circle at the point (-0.28, 0.96). Since cosine is the x-value and sine is the y-value, we can draw the following conclusion stated below.

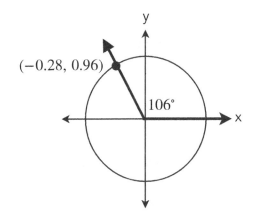

$$\cos 106° = -0.28, \ \sin 106° = 0.96$$

Angles greater than 90° or less than 0° have trigonometric ratios and these ratios can also be negative based on the quadrant.

 ## Range of Cosine & Sine

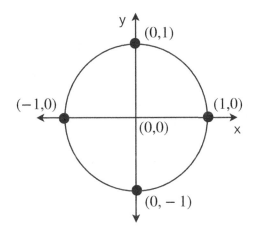

On the unit circle, the maximum x-value and y-value is 1 and the minimum x-value and y-value possible is -1.

Since cos & sin correspond with x & y, the ranges of x & y apply to cosine and sine as well. Therefore:

$$R_{\cos \theta} = [-1, \ 1] \quad R_{\sin \theta} = [-1, \ 1]$$

This means cos & sin of any angle can never be greater than 1 or less than -1.

NOTE

Remember that triangles sharing the same angle measure with different hypotenuses are similar. Therefore, even though the unit circle only shows right triangles with a hypotenuse of 1, the unit circle becomes a tool to depict trigonometric ratios for ANY right triangle.

Other Trigonometric Ratios

So far, we have looked at how to find cos & sin on the unit circle. To find the tangent ratio, we can divide $\sin \theta$ (the opposite side from θ) by $\cos \theta$ (the adjacent side near θ).
This provides a new, easier definition to find the tangent of ANY angle:

$$\tan \theta = \frac{\sin \theta}{\cos \theta} \qquad \tan \theta = \frac{y}{x}$$

In terms of the unit circle, this would be the y-value of the coordinate divided by the x-value.

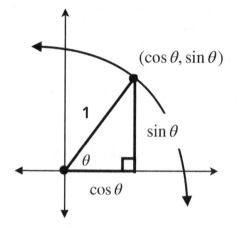

Similarly, to find the reciprocal ratios, we take the reciprocal of the x or y coordinates:

$$\cot \theta = \frac{\cos \theta}{\sin \theta} = \frac{x}{y} \qquad \csc \theta = \frac{1}{\sin \theta} = \frac{1}{y} \qquad \sec \theta = \frac{1}{\cos \theta} = \frac{1}{x}$$

 ## Example

Find all trigonometric ratios for π

Since π is a 180° rotation, this means the angle must intersect at the point (-1,0) on the unit circle.
If $x = -1$ and $y = 0$, then $\cos \pi = -1$ and $\sin \pi = 0$.
The remaining ratios are calculated below.

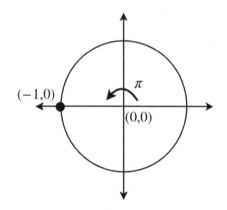

$$\sin \pi = 0 \qquad \csc \pi = \frac{1}{0} = \text{undefined}$$

$$\cos \pi = -1 \qquad \sec \pi = \frac{1}{-1} = -1$$

$$\tan \pi = \frac{0}{-1} = 0 \qquad \cot \pi = \frac{-1}{0} = \text{undefined}$$

3.3 Practice Problems

For #1-6, find the indicated ratio for the angle θ whose terminal side intersects with the given coordinate on the unit circle.

1 $(-0.5, 0.87)$

$\cos\theta$

2 $(0.79, 0.61)$

$\csc\theta$

3 $(0.1, -0.99)$

$\tan\theta$

4 $(1.01, 1.56)$

$\sin\theta$

5 $(-0.45, -0.89)$

$\cot\theta$

6 $(-0.91, 0.41)$

$\sec\theta$

For #7-9, find all 6 trigonometric ratios (sin, cos, tan, csc, sec, cot) for the given angle using the unit circle.

7 6π

8 $\dfrac{7\pi}{2}$

9 $\dfrac{17\pi}{2}$

Special Ratios on Unit Circle

In this lesson, we will extend our knowledge of the special ratios learned in lesson 2.6 by applying them to the unit circle.

Shown below are the simplified versions of the special triangles from lesson 2.6. However, these can only be applied to the unit circle if the hypotenuse is 1. So we will further simplify them by dividing all sides of both triangles by their hypotenuse ($\sqrt{2}$ for 45° and 2 for 30° and 60°).

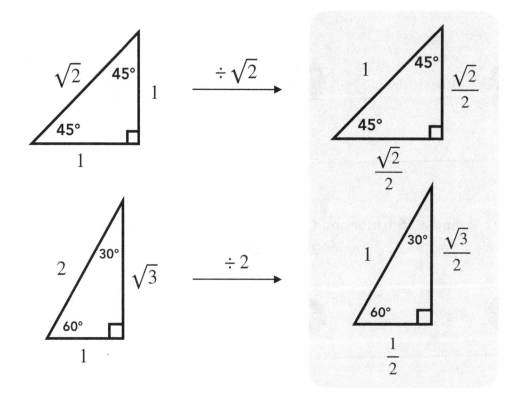

These triangles can then be represented on the unit circle as shown in the next example. However, since the hypotenuse is 1, the cosine and sine ratio for each angle is written as the leg of the triangle.

 **Example**   Find $\csc\left(\dfrac{\pi}{3}\right)$

It is important to be comfortable with using radians without needing to convert to degrees, but to help, the angle π/3 is the same as 60°. So, we can sketch a 60° angle on the first quadrant of the unit circle and label the legs using the new simplified triangles listed on the previous page.

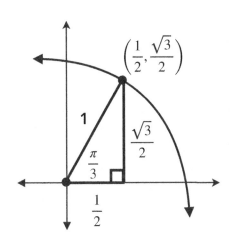

The y-value, which is $\dfrac{\sqrt{3}}{2}$, is the sine of the angle π/3

If cosecant is the same as $\dfrac{1}{\sin\theta}$, then $\csc\left(\dfrac{\pi}{3}\right) = \dfrac{1}{\frac{\sqrt{3}}{2}}$

$$\csc\left(\frac{\pi}{3}\right) = \frac{1}{\frac{\sqrt{3}}{2}} = \frac{2}{\sqrt{3}} \cdot \frac{\sqrt{3}}{\sqrt{3}} = \frac{2\sqrt{3}}{3}$$

TIP

Whenever sketching a triangle for 30° or 60° on the unit circle, the longer side is always $\dfrac{\sqrt{3}}{2}$ and the shorter side is $\dfrac{1}{2}$.

As noted before, angles such as $0, \dfrac{\pi}{2}, \pi, \dfrac{3\pi}{2}$, etc. have coordinates which are radius length (1) from the circle's center.

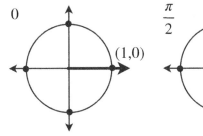
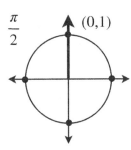
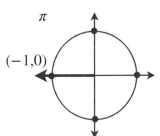
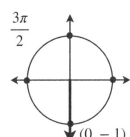

57

3.4 Practice Problems

Using the unit circle, evaluate the indicated trigonometric ratio for the following angles.

1 $\sin 30°$

2 $\cos 60°$

3 $\tan 45°$

4 $\cot 60°$

5 $\csc 45°$

6 $\sec 30°$

7 $\cos 45°$

8 $\cot 30°$

9 $\csc 60°$

3.5 Ratios of Any Angle

Throughout this unit, we have learned about the unit circle and how to find special trigonometric ratios in the first quadrant. We will now learn how to find the trigonometric ratio of any angle using all the knowledge we learned so far. To begin, let's learn another important vocabulary term.

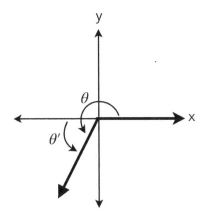

Reference Angle: An <u>acute positive</u> angle labeled as θ' which is formed by the x-axis and the terminal side.

Q **Example 1**   **Find the reference angle of 315°**

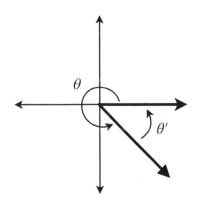

To find a reference angle, we can visually look at which quadrant the angle is placed in and determine the reference angle. In this case, subtracting 315° from 360° gives us the reference angle **45°**.

Reference angles help us re-create right triangles in different quadrants to help find the trigonometric ratios of any angle. Lets thoroughly examine how this works in the next example.

 **Example 2**   Find $\cot\left(\dfrac{7\pi}{6}\right)$

①

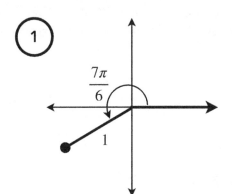

Always make a quick sketch of the radian angle on the <u>unit circle</u>.

②

Find the reference angle and make a triangle based from the x-axis with that reference angle. Since the angle is 7π/6 and the angle crosses π, then the reference angle must be $\dfrac{\pi}{6}$ (or 30°).

③

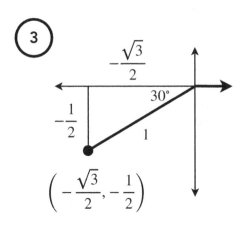

Let's now focus on only the 3rd quadrant. By knowing the reference angle, we can sketch a triangle in the 3rd quadrant lying on the unit circle. Since the hypotenuse is 1, we can fill the sides with the special ratios from the previous lesson. However, since this is <u>the third quadrant, the x & y values are negative</u>. This means the legs of the triangles are also written as **negative**.

④

$$\cot\left(\frac{7\pi}{6}\right) = \frac{-\frac{\sqrt{3}}{2}}{-\frac{1}{2}}\left(\frac{2}{2}\right) = \sqrt{3}$$

Since the actual angle and reference angle share the same coordinate, this means the angle $\dfrac{7\pi}{6}$ has the cosine value $-\dfrac{\sqrt{3}}{2}$ and the sine value $-\dfrac{1}{2}$. We can then use these to calculate the cotangent ratio.

Sign of Ratio

As you may have noticed in the last example, the quadrant, the angle lies in, determines whether or not the trigonometric ratio will be positive or negative.

The diagram to the right indicates which ratios are <u>positive</u> in each quadrant.

For example, wherever **x** is positive (Q1 & Q4), then **cosine** has to be positive; wherever **y** is negative (Q3 & Q4), then **sine** is negative.

<u>Note</u>: Tangent value is positive in Q3 because when sine value is negative and is divided by a negative cosine value, it results in a positive tangent ratio.

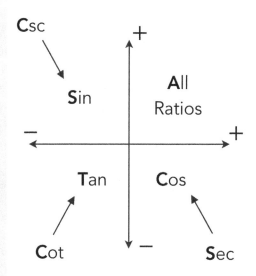

TIP

Here is a pneumonic to remember the positive ratios in each quadrant:

All **S**tudents **T**ake **C**alculus

Example 3

Find $\sin \theta$ if the terminal side of θ intersects (4,-6)

Begin by plotting (4,-6). Next, form a reference triangle with an angle θ' and find the legs (4 horizontally, -6 vertically). Although this point does not lie on the unit circle, the ratios remain the same. So, after finding the hypotenuse, $2\sqrt{13}$, we can calculate the sine of θ.

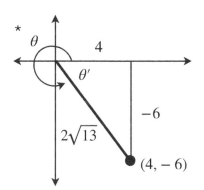

*For representation purposes, only one of the possible θ is shown.

$$\sin \theta = \frac{-6}{2\sqrt{13}} = -\frac{3\sqrt{13}}{13}$$

3.5 Practice Problems

For #1-9, evaluate the trigonometric ratio using the unit circle.

1 $\sin 300°$

2 $\cos\left(-\dfrac{3\pi}{4}\right)$

3 $\tan\left(\dfrac{4\pi}{3}\right)$

4 $\cot\left(\dfrac{5\pi}{6}\right)$

5 $\csc\left(-\dfrac{\pi}{3}\right)$

6 $\sec\left(-\dfrac{3\pi}{2}\right)$

7 $\cos\left(\dfrac{11\pi}{4}\right)$

8 $\sin(-720°)$

9 $\csc\left(\dfrac{13\pi}{6}\right)$

For #10-12, find the indicated ratio for the angle θ whose terminal side intersects with the given coordinate.

10 $(-7, -9)$

$\cos\theta$

11 $(-8, 5)$

$\tan\theta$

12 $(1, -6)$

$\csc\theta$

3.6 Trigonometric Equations

Using the concepts learned in the previous lesson to find trigonometric ratio of any angle, we can now apply these concepts in trigonometric equations to isolate an unknown variable.

Example 1 **In the equation below, solve for x in the domain $[0, 2\pi)$.**

The first step is to simplify the following equation into one trigonometric ratio.

$$\frac{2\sin x + 5}{3} = 2$$

$$\frac{2\sin x + 5}{3} = 2 \longrightarrow 2\sin x + 5 = 6 \longrightarrow 2\sin x = 1 \longrightarrow \sin x = \frac{1}{2}$$

Original Equation　　Multiply by 3 on both sides　　Subtract 5 on both sides　　Divide by 2 on both sides

From here, we must identify which angles have a sine ratio of positive $\frac{1}{2}$. The two quadrants where a sine ratio can be positive are Q1 and Q2. Knowing $\frac{\pi}{6}$ in Q1 retains this ratio, we can reflect its reference angle onto Q2 and notice that $\frac{5\pi}{6}$ shares this ratio as well. Keep in mind that these are the only two possible answers since the domain restricts to roots that are greater than or equal to 0 and less than 2π.

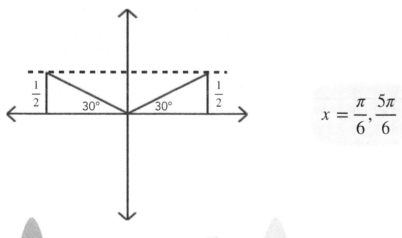

$$x = \frac{\pi}{6}, \frac{5\pi}{6}$$

The first step is to isolate $\cot^2(2x)$ in the equation and then simplify as shown below.

$$9\cot^2(2x) + 22 = 25$$

$$9\cot^2(2x) + 22 = 25 \rightarrow 9\cot^2(2x) = 3 \rightarrow \cot^2(2x) = \frac{1}{3} \rightarrow \cot(2x) = \pm\frac{1}{\sqrt{3}} \text{ or } \cot(2x) = \pm\frac{\sqrt{3}}{3}$$

| Original Equation | Subtract 22 on both sides | Divide by 9 on both sides | Square root on both sides | Rationalize denominator |

$$u = 2x \longrightarrow \cot(u) = \pm\frac{\sqrt{3}}{3}$$

Since square rooting both sides provides a positive and negative value for cotangent, this indicates that this ratio exists in all quadrants. Let's ignore 2x for now by substituting it for the variable 'u'. Using this, we can now try to find values of u that satisfy this equation.

If $\tan\theta = \frac{\sin\theta}{\cos\theta}$, then its reciprocal ratio, which is cotangent, must be $\cot\theta = \frac{\cos\theta}{\sin\theta}$.

Therefore, we can use the unit circle to find $\cot\frac{\pi}{3} = \frac{\frac{1}{2}}{\frac{\sqrt{3}}{2}} = \frac{1}{2} \cdot \frac{2}{\sqrt{3}} = \frac{1}{\sqrt{3}}$. By reflecting this

reference angle across all quadrants, the following values are concluded: $u = \frac{\pi}{3}, \frac{2\pi}{3}, \frac{4\pi}{3}, \frac{5\pi}{3}$

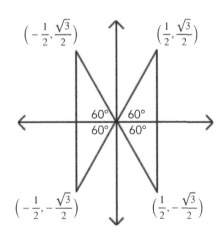

However, the problem asks to solve for x. Since u = 2x, substitute 2x back into the answers listed above and divide both sides of the equation by 2 to isolate for solutions of x.

$$2x = \frac{\pi}{3}, \frac{2\pi}{3}, \frac{4\pi}{3}, \frac{5\pi}{3} \longrightarrow x = \frac{\pi}{6}, \frac{\pi}{3}, \frac{2\pi}{3}, \frac{5\pi}{6}$$

3.6 Practice Problems

Solve the following trigonometric equations for x.
For #1-5, x must be in the domain $[0, 2\pi)$.
For #6, x must be in the domain $[0, \frac{\pi}{2})$.

1 $16\cos^2 x + 16\cos x + 4 = 0$

2 $3\sec^4 x + 2\sec^2 x = 8$

3 $\tan x \cos x - \tan x \sin x = 0$

4 $4\cot x = \dfrac{2(9\cot x + \sqrt{3})}{5}$

5 $7\tan^2 x - 5 = 23$

6 $12\sin^3(3x) = 6\sin(3x)$

Note: For #5, use calculator to solve.

66

Unit

4

Trigonometric Graphs

4.1 Sine & Cosine Graphs

Welcome to trigonometric graphs! In this unit, we apply the values of each trigonometric ratio and convert them into a <u>trigonometric function</u> that we can graph! Let's start this lesson by identifying the correct shape of a parent sine and cosine graph (also called sinusoidal functions).

 ## Sinusoidal Parent Functions

Before identifying the shape, we must label the axes. In trigonometric graphs, the **x-axis is the angle measurement (in radians)** and the **y-axis is the trigonometric ratio value** (ex. 1/2, 0, etc.)

We can use the table below to input some values in the function $f(x) = \sin(x)$ and identify the shape of the **parent** graph. The parent graph is the standard graph used for comparison when we perform transformations later.

Sin

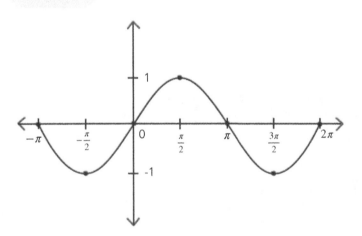

Cos

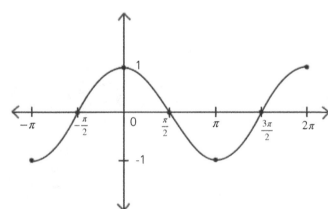

x	$-\pi$	$-\dfrac{\pi}{2}$	0	$\dfrac{\pi}{2}$	π	$\dfrac{3\pi}{2}$	2π
$f(x)$	0	-1	0	1	0	-1	0

x	$-\pi$	$-\dfrac{\pi}{2}$	0	$\dfrac{\pi}{2}$	π	$\dfrac{3\pi}{2}$	2π
$f(x)$	-1	0	1	0	-1	0	1

As we see in the above sinusoidal shape, sine and cosine graphs have a wave shape and they are identical except they are <u>shifted by $\dfrac{\pi}{2}$ units horizontally</u>. Also, all trigonometric functions are **periodic**, or repeat a continuous pattern/shape every **period**. This is because when we increase or decrease the angle measure, we begin to make multiple rotations around the unit circle, and this repeats the same trigonometric values.

Transformations & Properties

Here is a standard form for how sinusoidal functions are written, with each of the variables denoting a particular transformation or property of the parent function.

Standard Form

$$y = a\sin(b(x - c)) + d \quad \textbf{and} \quad y = a\cos(b(x - c)) + d$$

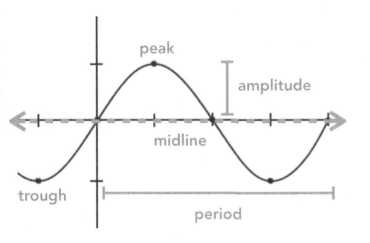

Amplitude: The height from the midline to peak or trough.

Period: The length of one complete cycle before the function repeats.

Midline: The line directly in the middle of the trough and peak.

Each of the variables a, b, c, and d in the standard form indicate the following:

a = amplitude (ex. |a| = 6 means amplitude is 6) If **a** is negative, there is a vertical reflection.

b = the number of cycles between 0 to 2π

To find the <u>period</u>, use the equation: period = $\dfrac{2\pi}{b}$ (ex. **b** = 3 means period is $\dfrac{2\pi}{3}$)

c = horizontally shifts function (ex. **c** = 3 means shift is 3 units right, **c** = -3 means 3 units left)

d = placement of midline (ex. **d** = 5 means the midline is y = 5)

Also remember the difference between the <u>parent graphs</u> of sine and cosine (before horizontal shifts). **Sine** will always cross or "start" from the origin and **cosine** will always have a peak/trough on the y-axis.

Example   **Graph the following function:** $f(x) = -2\cos(6x - \pi) + 2$

The first step is to convert this equation into standard form. In transformations, the horizontal shift only affects the value inside **x** and not the entire interior of $(6x - \pi)$. To convert to standard form, we simply factor the 6 inside the cosine to have values a, b, c, and d.

$$f(x) = -2\cos(6x - \pi) + 2 \quad \longrightarrow \quad f(x) = -2\cos\left(6\left(x - \frac{\pi}{6}\right)\right) + 2$$

The next step is to identify amplitude, period, horizontal shift, vertical reflection, & midline. First, we can acquire the following values from the equation above:
$a = -2$, $b = 6$, $c = \frac{\pi}{6}$, $d = 2$.

- The amplitude is defined as |a|, so the amplitude is 2.
- Since a is negative, there is a vertical reflection.
- The period uses b in the formula $\frac{2\pi}{b}$, so the period is $\frac{\pi}{3}$.
- The horizontal shift is **c** and since it is positive, the function shifts $\frac{\pi}{6}$ to the right.
- The vertical shift is **d** and since it is positive, the function shifts up by 2.

Amplitude: 2

Period: $\frac{2\pi}{b} = \frac{2\pi}{6} = \frac{\pi}{3}$

Horizontal Shift: $\frac{\pi}{6}$ right

Vertical Shift: 2 up

Vertical Reflection: yes

Midline: y = 2

We can graph this function by scaling the x-axis by $\frac{\pi}{12}$. Leave space to graph 1.5 to 2 periods. Let's graph this function using 3 steps shown below.

①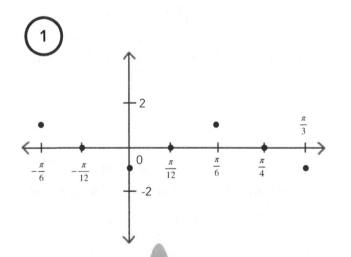

Only plot points with the period $\frac{\pi}{3}$ and vertical reflection (i.e. graph $y = -\cos(6x)$).

Remember that **cosine** starts with a peak or trough on the y-axis. Using the increments on the x-axis, you can already define where points are located since each period has 5 **significant points**.

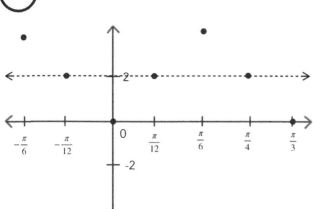

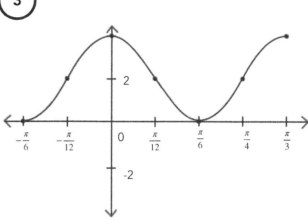

Transform Graph 1 by increasing the amplitude to 2 and shifting to midline y=2.

(i.e. graph $y = -2\cos(6x) + 2$)

Shift all points to the right by $\dfrac{\pi}{6}$ units

(i.e. graph $f(x) = -2\cos(6x - \pi) + 2$)

TIP!

To help scale the x-axis, notice how each of these graphs have <u>5 major significant points</u> in each period, dividing the period into "4 sections".

So, you can find the **quarter** by dividing the period (ex. $\dfrac{\pi}{3}$) by 4 (i.e. $\dfrac{\pi}{12}$) and this is how you can scale/interval the x-axis.

4.1 Practice Problems

For each of the functions below, write the period, amplitude, vertical reflection, midline, and horizontal shift. Then, graph the function as well.

1 $f(x) = -\sin\left(\dfrac{1}{4}x\right) + 1$

2 $f(x) = 3\cos(4x + 2\pi) - 2$

3 $f(x) = -2\cos\left(\dfrac{5x}{3} + \dfrac{2\pi}{3}\right)$

4 $f(x) = \dfrac{3}{2}\sin(6x - 5\pi) + \dfrac{1}{2}$

5 $h(x) = -\dfrac{\pi}{2}\sin\left(\pi x - \dfrac{5\pi}{2}\right) - 2\pi$

6 $g(x) = 8\cos\left(3\left(x - \dfrac{\pi}{3}\right)\right)$

7 $g(x) = -4\cos\left(\dfrac{8}{5}x + 4\pi\right) + 6$

8 $h(x) = 3\sin(8x - 5\pi) - 4$

4.2 Tangent & Cotangent Graphs

As we continue to explore trigonometric graphs further, in this lesson we will learn about tangent and cotangent graphs. Keep in mind that these functions do not behave like a wave since they have distinct properties compared to sine or cosine.

 Tangent & Cotangent Parent Functions

Let's try to understand the shape of these graphs by inputting values for **x** as shown in the table below.

Tan

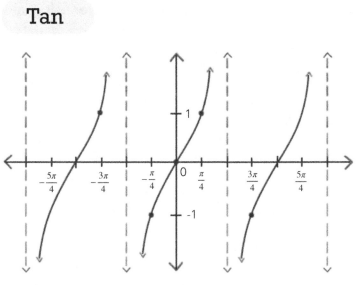

Cot

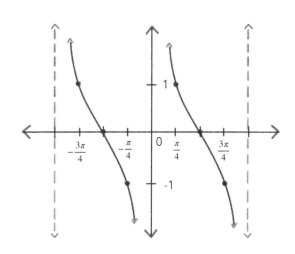

x	$-\dfrac{3\pi}{4}$	$-\dfrac{\pi}{2}$	$-\dfrac{\pi}{4}$	0	$\dfrac{\pi}{4}$	$\dfrac{\pi}{2}$	$\dfrac{3\pi}{4}$
$f(x)$	1	undef	-1	0	1	undef	-1

x	$-\dfrac{3\pi}{4}$	$-\dfrac{\pi}{2}$	$-\dfrac{\pi}{4}$	0	$\dfrac{\pi}{4}$	$\dfrac{\pi}{2}$	$\dfrac{3\pi}{4}$
$f(x)$	1	0	-1	undef	1	0	-1

Tangent and cotangent are periodic functions that repeat in a continuous cycle. Notice how these graphs have **asymptotes**, or lines that the function approaches due to a particular x-value being undefined. Additionally, the cotangent and tangent functions are vertical reflections of one another translated by $\dfrac{\pi}{2}$ units horizontally.

Transformations & Properties

Here is a standard form for trigonometric functions which behaves very similar to the standard form of sinusoidal functions.

Standard Form

$$y = a \tan(b(x - c)) + d \quad \textbf{and} \quad y = a \cot(b(x - c)) + d$$

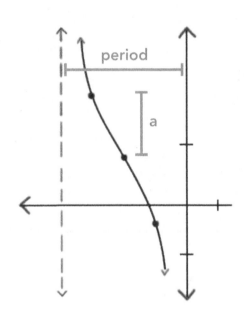

a = vertically stretches the function from the center using lal

b = the number of cycles between 0 to π
To find the <u>period</u>, use the equation: period $= \dfrac{\pi}{b}$

c = horizontally shifts function

d = vertically shifts function

Remember the difference between the <u>parent graphs</u> of tangent and cotangent (before any transformation).

As $x \to \infty$, **tangent** will approach ∞ (+ on left end, - on right end) and **cotangent** will approach $-\infty$ (- on left end, + on right end).

To remember the graph's position from one another, **tangent** has some asymptotes on $x = -\dfrac{\pi}{2}, \dfrac{\pi}{2}$ while **cotangent** has some asymptotes on $x = 0, \pi$.

Example

Graph the following function: $f(x) = 3\tan(2x + \dfrac{3\pi}{4}) - 1$

Similar to transformations in other functions, the first step is to convert this function into a standard form by factoring the 2 inside $(2x - 3\pi)$.

$$f(x) = 3\tan(2x + \frac{3\pi}{4}) - 1 \longrightarrow f(x) = 3\tan\left(2\left(x + \frac{3\pi}{8}\right)\right) - 1$$

The next step is to identify period, horizontal shift, vertical reflection, vertical shift, vertical stretch. First, we can acquire the following values from the equation above:

$a = 3$, $b = 2$, $c = -\dfrac{3\pi}{8}$, $d = -1$.

- Vertical stretch is defined as lal, so vertical stretch is 3.
- Since a is positive, there is no vertical reflection.
- The period uses b in the formula $\dfrac{\pi}{b}$, so the period is $\dfrac{\pi}{2}$.
- The horizontal shift is **c** and since it is negative, the function shifts $\dfrac{3\pi}{8}$ to the left.
- The vertical shift is **d** and since it is negative, the function shifts down by 1.

Period: $\dfrac{\pi}{b} = \dfrac{\pi}{2}$

Horizontal Shift: $\dfrac{3\pi}{8}$ left

Vertical Reflection: no

Vertical Shift: 1 down

Vertical Stretch: 3

Using this information, we can now graph our function. Setup the graph using a <u>quarter</u> increment of $\dfrac{\pi}{8}$ as the scale for the x-axis, having 2 full periods. Let's graph this in 3 steps.

①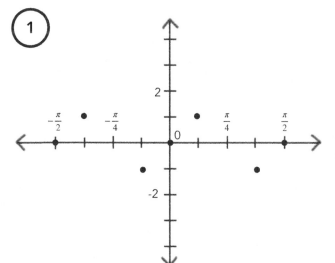

First graph only the points based on the period (one cycle) which is $\dfrac{\pi}{2}$ (i.e. $y = \tan(2x)$).

Remember tangent starts from the origin and goes up to the right and down to the left. Use this as a reference to graph three significant points per period. Leave a gap of one increment to fill with an asymptote later!

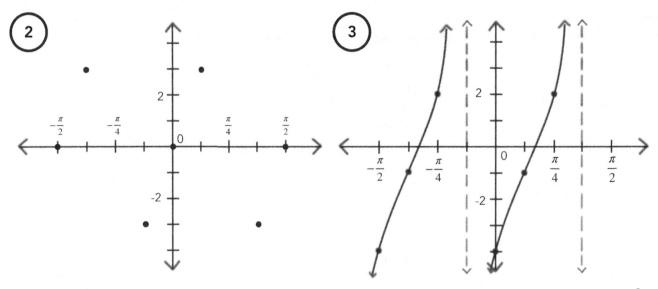

2

3

Next, vertically stretch this function by 3. The a-value (3) is the vertical distance of adjacent points from the middle point of the tangent curve.

Finally, shift all the points 1 unit down and $\dfrac{3\pi}{8}$ units to the left. Fill the remaining blank increments with an asymptote.

$$(\text{i.e. } f(x) = 3\tan\left(2\left(x + \frac{3\pi}{8}\right)\right) - 1)$$

Equation of Asymptotes

Whenever describing any function with periodic asymptotes, we must create a <u>rule</u> for the asymptote locations denoted as an equation since an infinite number of asymptotes can be listed. The equation below shows how to write a rule for every periodic asymptote of a tangent or cotangent function:

Formula to Write the Rule of Periodic Asymptotes for Tangent & Cotangent

$$x = m + kn$$

m = the first positive asymptote nearest to or on the y-axis
n = can be any integer
k = period of the function

Let's apply this rule for our previous example. Since the period of f(x) is $\dfrac{\pi}{2}$, the **k** value must also be $\dfrac{\pi}{2}$. Therefore, the distance between the two asymptotes is defined as $\dfrac{\pi}{2}$. Next, we must find the first positive asymptote closest to the y-axis, which for this example is $x = \dfrac{3\pi}{8}$. Using all of this information, the final asymptote equation is denoted as: $x = \dfrac{3\pi}{8} + \dfrac{\pi}{2}n$.

In summary, this rule states that every **n**th time $\dfrac{\pi}{2}$ units precede or follow $x = \dfrac{3\pi}{8}$, f(x) must have an asymptote at that x-value.

4.2 Practice Problems

For each of the functions below, write the period, vertical reflection & stretch, vertical shift, and horizontal shift. Graph the function and write the rule for asymptotes as well.

1 $f(x) = -3\tan\left(\dfrac{3}{2}x\right) + 2$

2 $f(x) = 5\cot(6x + 2\pi) - 1$

3 $f(x) = -4\cot\left(\dfrac{7x}{2} + \dfrac{\pi}{2}\right)$

4 $f(x) = \dfrac{5}{4}\tan(4x - \pi) + \dfrac{5}{2}$

5 $h(x) = -\dfrac{5\pi}{2}\tan\left(\dfrac{\pi x}{8} - \dfrac{\pi}{4}\right) - \pi$

6 $g(x) = 5\cot\left(\dfrac{6}{7}\left(x - \dfrac{\pi}{3}\right)\right)$

7 $g(x) = -3\cot\left(\dfrac{3}{4}x + \dfrac{9\pi}{2}\right) + 1$

8 $h(x) = 9\tan\left(4x - \dfrac{5\pi}{2}\right) - 4$

After covering the graphs for 4 of the 6 trigonometric ratios, in this lesson, we will focus on how to graph the cosecant and secant functions. Throughout this lesson, we will discuss how these functions share a common relationship with the sine and cosine functions we learned before.

 ## Cosecant & Secant Shape

Let's try to understand the shape of these graphs by inputting some values for **x** as shown in the table below.

Csc

Sec

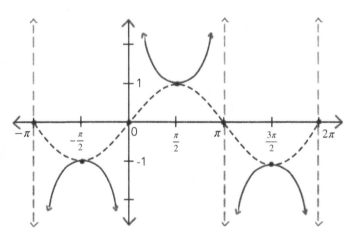

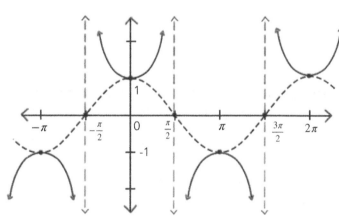

x	$-\pi$	$-\dfrac{\pi}{2}$	0	$\dfrac{\pi}{2}$	π	$\dfrac{3\pi}{2}$	2π
$f(x)$	undef	-1	undef	1	undef	-1	undef

x	$-\pi$	$-\dfrac{\pi}{2}$	0	$\dfrac{\pi}{2}$	π	$\dfrac{3\pi}{2}$	2π
$f(x)$	-1	undef	1	undef	-1	undef	1

Cosecant and secant functions are periodic and contain vertical <u>asymptotes</u>, similar to tangent and cotangent functions. However, as shown in the above graphs, these functions follow the pattern of their reciprocal functions sine and cosine which are elaborated in the next section.

Relationships with Sine & Cosine

Sine and cosine are closely related to cosecant and secant respectively since they are reciprocals of one another. Let's analyze the graphs from the previous page.

Recall $\csc x = \dfrac{1}{\sin x}$ and $\sec x = \dfrac{1}{\cos x}$. Using this, there are 3 conclusions we can draw:

1) A point exists on each peak and trough of the sine and cosine graphs. This is because the reciprocal of -1 or 1 remains the same.

2) Asymptotes exist at the x-intercepts of sine and cosine graphs because when sin(x) = 0 or cos(x) = 0, the denominator of csc and sec become 0 as well making the function undefined.

3) The graph approaches ∞ and −∞ because the values of sine and cosine are restricted between 0 and 1 and reciprocals of these fractional values result in large numbers.

From these patterns, we can conclude that whenever we graph, we should convert the cosecant or secant graph into a sine or cosine function. This allows us to first graph significant points as reference, which then enables us to shape the cosecant or secant graph later on.

Remember once again that the period of a cosecant or secant function is $\dfrac{2\pi}{b}$

First, start by converting this function into the reciprocal sine function $g(x)$ and graph $g(x)$ normally with a dotted line. Make sure to still identify the period, vertical shift, horizontal shift, vertical reflection if necessary.

$$f(x) = 2\csc(5x + 3\pi) - 3 \quad \longrightarrow \quad g(x) = 2\sin(5x + 3\pi) - 3$$

Period: $\dfrac{2\pi}{b} = \dfrac{2\pi}{5}$

Horizontal Shift: $\dfrac{3\pi}{5}$ left

Vertical Reflection: no

Vertical Shift: 3 down

Vertical Stretch: 2

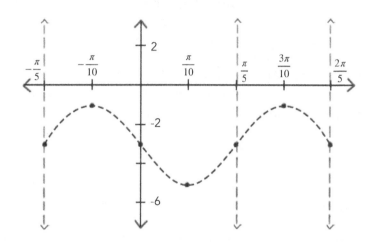

Before the vertical shift, asymptotes would have been located on points lying directly on the x-axis. But since this function has been shifted down by 3 units, the asymptotes now intersect points directly on the **midline** $y = -3$. This is why the asymptotes are drawn as such.

To make the actual function, remember the peaks of this sine graph are the relative minimums of the "U" shaped cosecant curves, and the troughs of this sine graph are the relative maximums. Remember to make these curves approach the vertical asymptotes. The graph on the next page illustrates this.

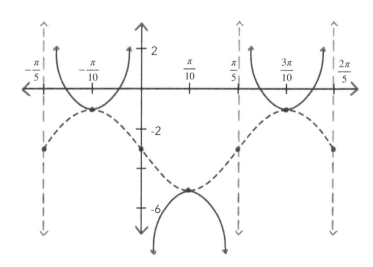

Equation of Asymptotes

Similar to the cotangent and tangent functions in the previous lesson, we must create a rule for the asymptote locations denoted as an equation since an infinite number of asymptotes can be listed. The equation below shows how to write a rule for every periodic asymptote of a cosecant or secant function:

Formula to Write the Rule of Periodic Asymptotes for Cosecant & Secant

$$x = m + kn$$

m = the first positive asymptote nearest to or on the y-axis
n = can be any integer
k = period of the function <u>divided by 2</u>

Let's apply this rule for our previous example. Since the period of f(x) is $\frac{2\pi}{5}$, the **k** value must also be $\frac{2\pi}{5} \div 2$, which is $\frac{\pi}{5}$. Therefore, the distance between the two asymptotes is defined as $\frac{\pi}{5}$. Next, we must find the first positive asymptote closest to the y-axis, which for this example is $x = 0$ as it lies directly on the y-axis. Using all of this information, the final asymptote equation is denoted as: $x = \frac{\pi}{5}n$.

In summary, this rule states that every **nth** time $\frac{\pi}{5}$ units precede or follow the y-axis, f(x) must have an asymptote at that x-value.

4.3 Practice Problems

For each of the functions below, write the period, vertical reflection & stretch, vertical shift, and horizontal shift. Graph the function and write the rule for asymptotes as well.

1 $f(x) = -\csc\left(\frac{2}{3}x\right) + 3$

2 $f(x) = 2\sec(2x + 3\pi) - 4$

3 $f(x) = -2\sec\left(\frac{x}{4} + \frac{3\pi}{4}\right)$

4 $f(x) = \frac{2}{3}\csc(4x - \pi) + \frac{1}{3}$

5 $h(x) = -\frac{\pi}{2}\csc\left(2\pi x - 3\pi\right) - \pi$

6 $g(x) = 2\sec\left(4\left(x - \frac{5\pi}{4}\right)\right)$

7 $g(x) = -3\sec\left(\frac{7}{4}x + 3\pi\right) + 5$

8 $h(x) = 3\csc\left(6x + \frac{\pi}{2}\right) - 1$

4.4 Equations from Graphs

After graphing all of the standard trigonometric graphs for all 6 ratios, let's now practice going backwards - learn how to identify the function, given the picture of a graph.

Before we view some examples to understand this better, keep a few things in mind:

1. Cotangent & tangent, cosecant & secant, and sine & cosine are each translations of one another and the same graph can be written as 2 different functions.
   (ex. $\sin(x) = \cos\left(x - \dfrac{\pi}{2}\right)$).
2. Focus on finding the function's transformations and matching them with the specific variables in their standard form.

Q **Example**   **Find the tangent function $f(x)$ and cotangent function $g(x)$ of the graph shown below.**

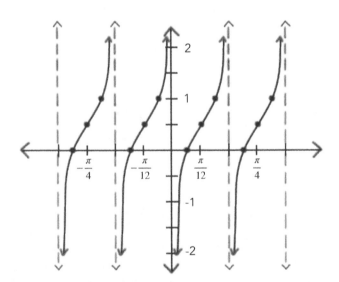

To start, we can already deduce values of **a** and **b** based on the period and vertical stretch.

The vertical stretch from the middle point of a curve to its adjacent point is $\dfrac{1}{2}$, so $a = \dfrac{1}{2}$.

Moreover, the period of the function is $\dfrac{\pi}{6}$, so if $\dfrac{\pi}{b} = \dfrac{\pi}{6}$ (the period), then $b = 6$.

So far, our function in terms of cotangent and tangent is $f(x) = \dfrac{1}{2}\tan(6x)$ & $g(x) = \dfrac{1}{2}\cot(6x)$.

To find values of **c** (horizontal shift), **d** (vertical shift), and vertical reflection, we must picture a general outline of a tangent or cotangent parent graph to observe the transformations accordingly. Let's first start with the tangent parent graph shown below.

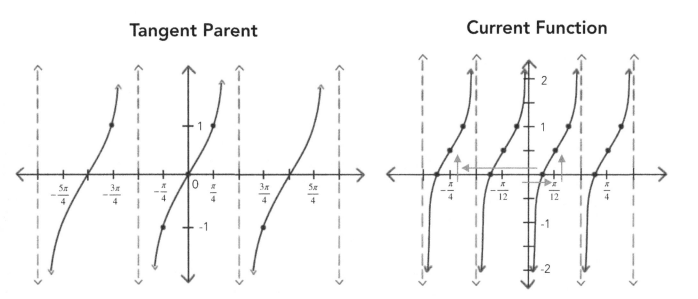

Tangent Parent   **Current Function**

Since the end behavior of both graphs are the same, there is no vertical reflection. However, the first middle point (using for reference) in the parent graph which is (0,0) appears to have shifted in either two possible directions: right $\dfrac{\pi}{12}$ & up $\dfrac{1}{2}$ **or** left $\dfrac{\pi}{4}$ & up $\dfrac{1}{2}$

Since both translations are possibilities, we can write either tangent function for our answer (for clarification purposes, both answers are written but only one final answer is needed). Keep in mind that many translations are possible aside from the two identified above and therefore, answers may vary.

If right $\dfrac{\pi}{12}$ & up $\dfrac{1}{2}$, $c = \dfrac{\pi}{12}$ & $d = \dfrac{1}{2}$:

$$f(x) = \frac{1}{2} \tan\left(6\left(x - \frac{\pi}{12}\right)\right) + \frac{1}{2}$$

$$\boxed{f(x) = \frac{1}{2} \tan\left(6x - \frac{\pi}{2}\right) + \frac{1}{2}}$$

If left $\dfrac{\pi}{4}$ & up $\dfrac{1}{2}$, $c = -\dfrac{\pi}{4}$ & $d = \dfrac{1}{2}$:

$$g(x) = \frac{1}{2} \tan\left(6\left(x + \frac{\pi}{4}\right)\right) + \frac{1}{2}$$

$$\boxed{g(x) = \frac{1}{2} \tan\left(6x + \frac{3\pi}{2}\right) + \frac{1}{2}}$$

Now that we have found the function in terms of tangent, let's look at this with the perspective of cotangent. Below are both the cotangent parent graph and current graph.

Cotangent Parent

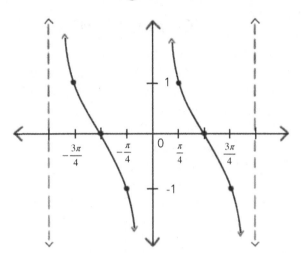

Current Function

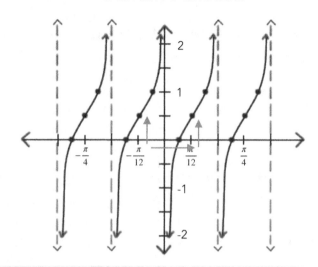

The end behavior of both graphs is opposite, so there is a vertical reflection here meaning: **a is negative**. Although there is a difference in period, one of the transformations will only consist of moving up by $\frac{1}{2}$, since the function is horizontally scaled without horizontally shifting it. Another possible transformation is to scale $\left(\frac{\pi}{2}, 0\right)$ on the parent graph and shift it right $\frac{\pi}{6}$ & up $\frac{1}{2}$. Keep in mind that since both translations are possibilities, they can be written as either cotangent function and therefore, their answers may vary.

If up $\frac{1}{2}$, $c = 0$ & $d = \frac{1}{2}$:

$$g(x) = -\frac{1}{2}\cot(6x) + \frac{1}{2}$$

If right $\frac{\pi}{6}$ & up $\frac{1}{2}$, $c = \frac{\pi}{6}$ & $d = \frac{1}{2}$:

$$g(x) = -\frac{1}{2}\cot\left(6\left(x - \frac{\pi}{6}\right)\right) + \frac{1}{2}$$

$$g(x) = -\frac{1}{2}\cot(6x - \pi) + \frac{1}{2}$$

See how many ways we can graph the __same periodic function__! Although the above example relates to tan & cot, we can follow similar steps for the other trigonometric functions as well. Always remember to check your work by graphing your answer(s) on a graphing utility and see if they overlap or match the graph provided in the problem.

4.4 Practice Problems

Identify the function in each of the following graphs in terms of sin OR cos, tan OR cot, or csc OR sec.

1

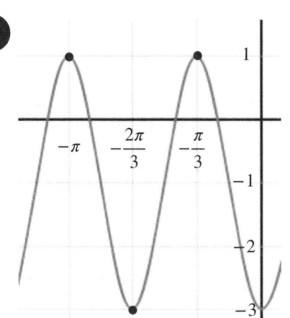

2

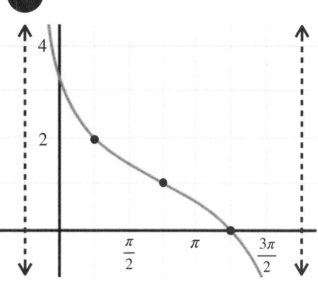

3

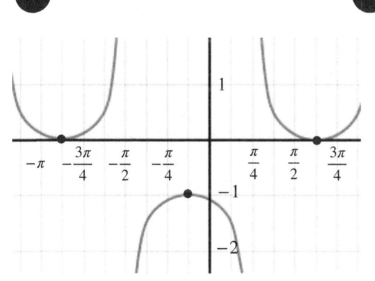

4

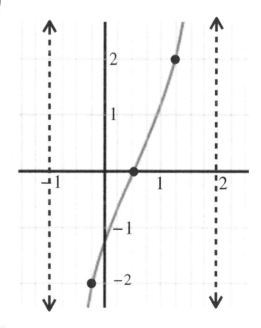

4.5 Inverse Trigonometric Graphs

In the previous lessons, we learned about the 6 trigonometric graphs and their behavior. We will now expand upon the concepts taught in lesson 2.4 on inverse trigonometry and how to graph inverse trigonometric functions.

 Inverse Trigonometry Review & Graph

Inverse trigonometry is the **inverse** of a standard trigonometric function. We input a trigonometric value and the function outputs the angle measurements that share this trigonometric value. This is why inverse trigonometric functions are opposite of functions we have learned so far. Here the x-values will be the trigonometric values and the y-values will be angles in radians. For example, for $f(x) = \arcsin(x)$ or $f(x) = \sin^{-1}(x)$, $f\left(\dfrac{1}{2}\right) = \dfrac{\pi}{6}$.

Note that the inverse of a function corresponds to its inverse trigonometric ratio.
For example, the inverse of $f(x) = \tan(x)$ is $f^{-1}(x) = \tan^{-1}(x)$. Since $f(x)$ and $f^{-1}(x)$ are always reflections of one another over the line y = x, this means $\tan(x)$ and $\tan^{-1}(x)$ are also reflections over the line y = x, meaning they share the same shape but are simply "rotated".

This pattern can be seen in the following parent inverse trigonometric graphs shown below.

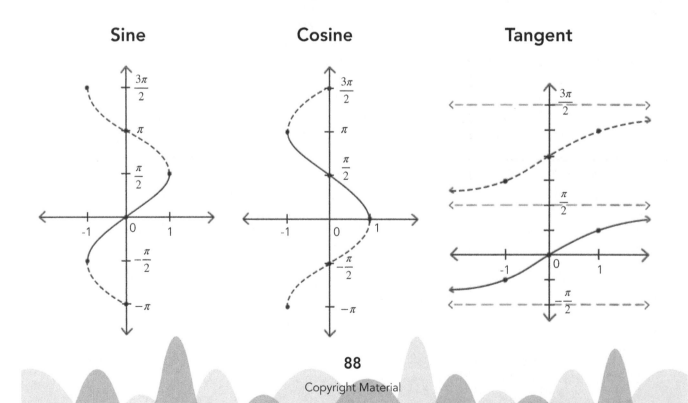

Sine   **Cosine**   **Tangent**

Inverse Graph Shape

Let's reference the graphs on the previous page. You may have noticed that some parts of the curve are dotted

Standard trigonometric functions are periodic and continue to cycle along the x-axis. Similarly, inverse trigonometric functions would ideally cycle along the y-axis. However, since these graphs are <u>functions</u>, **one input** must only match with **one output**.

This can be tested using the **Vertical Line Test** by drawing a vertical line through any portion of the graph and checking to see if the line intersects <u>only at one point</u>.

In the diagram to the right, a line drawn through the middle intersects at two points, failing the vertical line test. This indicates it is not a function.

In order to make this inverse a function and pass the Vertical Line Test, the **range must only be restricted to the solid**

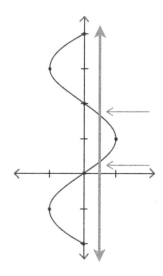

Listed below are the restricted ranges (or y-values) that are used for graphing inverse functions. Values within this range (unless vertically stretched or shifted) are the only values graphed.

Arcsine is restricted between the range $\left[\dfrac{\pi}{2}, -\dfrac{\pi}{2}\right]$

Arccosine is restricted between the range $[0, \pi]$

Arctangent is restricted between the range $\left(\dfrac{\pi}{2}, -\dfrac{\pi}{2}\right)$

Reminder that the prefix "arc" is the same as denoting -1 on a function. So $\arctan(x)$ is the same as writing $\tan^{-1}(x)$.

NOTE

Example   **Graph the following function:** $f(x) = -2\cos^{-1}(2x+2) + \dfrac{\pi}{2}$

Similar to other function transformations, the first step is to convert this function into the "standard" form so it can be analyzed later.

$$f(x) = -2\cos^{-1}(2x+2) + \frac{\pi}{2} \quad\longrightarrow\quad f(x) = -2\cos^{-1}(2(x+1)) + \frac{\pi}{2}$$

Then, identify the function transformations accordingly.

Horizontal Stretch: Since **x** is multiplied by a factor of 2, the function shrinks by $\dfrac{1}{2}$

Horizontal Shift: 1 left   **Vertical Reflection:** yes

Vertical Shift: $\dfrac{\pi}{2}$ up   **Vertical Stretch:** 3

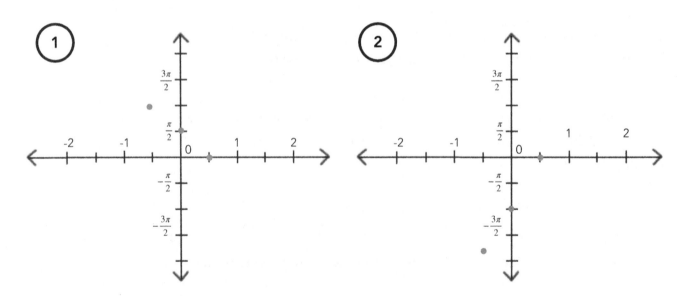

Plot the parent arccosine graph with the restricted domain and stretch it by $\dfrac{1}{2}$ horizontally from the y-axis.
(i.e. $y = \cos^{-1}(2x)$)

Vertically stretch this function from the x-axis by multiplying each point's y-value by 2. Reflect these points across the x-axis as well.
(i.e. $y = -2\cos^{-1}(2x)$)

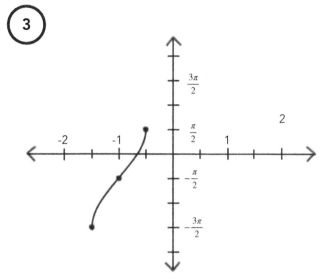

Shift all points up by $\dfrac{\pi}{2}$ units and to the left by 1 unit

$$\text{(i.e. } f(x) = -2\cos^{-1}(2(x+1)) + \frac{\pi}{2})$$

4.5 Practice Problems

For each of the functions below, write the period, vertical reflection & stretch, vertical shift, and horizontal shift. Graph the function and write the correct domain & range.

1 $f(x) = \sin^{-1}\left(\dfrac{4}{5}x\right) + 2$

2 $f(x) = \dfrac{2}{3}\arccos(3x + 3) - \dfrac{4\pi}{3}$

3 $f(x) = -2\tan^{-1}\left(\dfrac{x}{4} + \dfrac{3}{4}\right)$

4 $f(x) = \dfrac{1}{3}\cos^{-1}\left(\dfrac{4}{\pi}x - 4\right) - 2$

5 $h(x) = -\dfrac{1}{3\pi}\sin^{-1}\left(2x - 4\right) - 1$

6 $g(x) = 3\arctan\left(7\left(x - \dfrac{4\pi}{7}\right)\right)$

7 $g(x) = -3\arcsin(x + 3) + \dfrac{7\pi}{4}$

8 $h(x) = 4\cos^{-1}\left(\dfrac{1}{4}x - 1\right) + 2\pi$

Unit

5

Applications of Trigonometry

5.1 More Inverse Trigonometry

Welcome to a new unit! Here we will see how the trigonometric knowledge learned from the unit circle and graphs can be applied to standard triangle problems. We will also use the inverse trigonometric graphs to look at inverse trigonometry problems with a different perspective.

 ## Domain & Range

Since we have viewed inverse trigonometry as functions with restricted range, we must apply this same concept to regular inverse trigonometric problems. Listed below are ranges for each ratio depicted on the unit circle as well as on each corresponding domain:

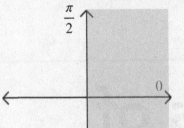

Arcsine $(\sin^{-1} x)$

Domain: $[-1, 1]$

Range: $\left[-\dfrac{\pi}{2}, \dfrac{\pi}{2} \right]$

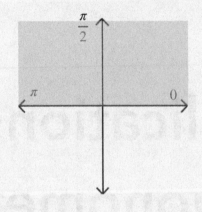

Arccosine $(\cos^{-1} x)$

Domain: $[-1, 1]$

Range: $[0, \pi]$

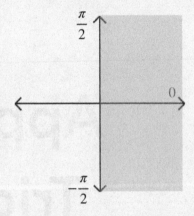

Arctangent $(\tan^{-1} x)$

Domain: $(-\infty, \infty)$

Range: $\left(-\dfrac{\pi}{2}, \dfrac{\pi}{2} \right)$

To remember these range restrictions, simply picture the parent graphs and identify the maximum and minimum x & y values. For tangent, keep in mind that the maximum and minimum values are right below the asymptotes, so everything within the range except for the asymptote values are included. Additionally, tangent extends infinitely horizontally in both directions.

Example 1   **Evaluate the following inverse trigonometric ratios.**

1 $\cos^{-1}\left(\dfrac{\sqrt{2}}{2}\right)$

  $\arctan(-\sqrt{3})$

The only reference angle that can have such a cosine ratio is $\dfrac{\pi}{4}$.

To have a positive cosine ratio, the angle must be located in Q1 or Q4 since these are quadrants where **x** is positive.

Since the range of cosine is between Q1 & Q2, we must place the reference angle in Q1. This means the actual angle from the initial side must be $\dfrac{\pi}{4}$.

This ratio requires an absolute sine value of $\dfrac{\sqrt{3}}{2}$ and absolute cosine value of $\dfrac{1}{2}$.

On the unit circle, this graph creates a reference angle of $\dfrac{\pi}{3}$.
A negative tangent ratio can exist in Q2 or Q4, but tangent restricts its range within Q1 & Q4. So, the reference angle must be placed in Q4, indicating the angle is $-\dfrac{\pi}{3}$.

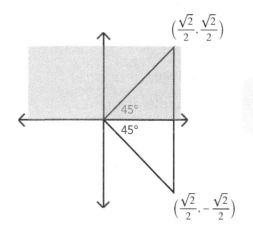

$\dfrac{\pi}{4}$

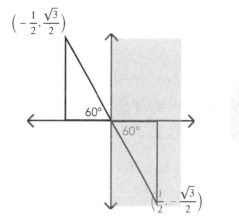

$-\dfrac{\pi}{3}$

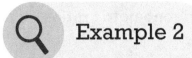 **Example 2** **Evaluate the expression:** $\csc(\arccos(0))$

To solve expressions combined with inverse and non-inverse functions, start with the embedded expression $\arccos(0)$. We must find the angle where cosine is 0 in the restricted range $[0, \pi]$. Using the unit circle, this angle would be $\dfrac{\pi}{2}$ which reduces the expression to $\csc\left(\dfrac{\pi}{2}\right)$.

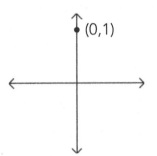

Evaluate the cosecant

$$\csc\left(\frac{\pi}{2}\right) = \frac{1}{\sin\left(\frac{\pi}{2}\right)} = \frac{1}{1} = 1 \longrightarrow \csc(\arccos(0)) = 1$$

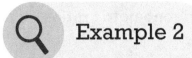 **Example 3** **Simplify the expression:** $\tan\left(\sin^{-1}\left(\dfrac{2}{5x-4}\right)\right)$

In this problem, we need to first focus on the embedded expression $\sin^{-1}\left(\dfrac{2}{5x-4}\right)$. Since no numerical values are provided, we must create our own triangle diagram assuming that an arbitrary angle θ has a sine of $\dfrac{2}{5x-4}$. Since sine is the opposite side of θ divided by the hypotenuse, the opposite side of θ will be 2 and the hypotenuse side of this triangle will be $5x - 4$.

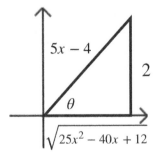

Find the **adjacent** side using Pythagorean Theorem.

$$\sqrt{(5x-4)^2 - 2^2} = \sqrt{25x^2 - 40x + 16 - 4} = \sqrt{25x^2 - 40x + 12}$$

Evaluate the tangent ratio of θ

$$\tan(\theta) = \frac{2}{\sqrt{25x^2 - 40x + 12}} \cdot \frac{\sqrt{25x^2 - 40x + 12}}{\sqrt{25x^2 - 40x + 12}} = \frac{2\sqrt{25x^2 - 40x + 12}}{25x^2 - 40x + 12}$$

$$\tan\left(\sin^{-1}\left(\frac{2}{5x - 4}\right)\right) = \frac{2\sqrt{25x^2 - 40x + 12}}{25x^2 - 40x + 12}$$

Domain & Range of Reciprocal Ratios

In addition, the reciprocal functions $\csc(x)$, $\sec(x)$, or $\cot(x)$ have the corresponding inverse functions: $\csc^{-1}(x)$, $\sec^{-1}(x)$, and $\cot^{-1}(x)$.

Listed below are the domains and ranges of each function:

Arc-cosecant $(\csc^{-1} x)$

Domain: $(-\infty, -1] \cup [1, \infty)$

Range: $\left[-\frac{\pi}{2}, 0\right) \cup \left(0, \frac{\pi}{2}\right]$

Arc-secant $(\sec^{-1} x)$

Domain: $(-\infty, -1] \cup [1, \infty)$

Range: $\left[0, \frac{\pi}{2}\right) \cup \left(\frac{\pi}{2}, \pi\right]$

Arc-cotangent $(\cot^{-1} x)$

Domain: $(-\infty, \infty)$

Range: $(0, \pi)$

5.1 Practice Problems

Evaluate each of the following expression.

1 $\sin^{-1}\left(-\dfrac{\sqrt{3}}{2}\right)$

2 $\arctan\left(\dfrac{\sqrt{3}}{3}\right)$

3 $\sec^{-1}\left(-\sqrt{2}\right)$

4 $\csc^{-1}(2)$

5 $\sin\left(\arctan\left(-\sqrt{3}\right)\right)$

6 $\cot(-\cos^{-1}(0.75))$

7 $\tan\left(\sin^{-1}\left(\dfrac{5x-6}{7x+4}\right)\right)$

8 $\sin\left(\sec^{-1}\left(-\dfrac{2}{x-3}\right)\right)$

5.2 Law of Sines

The next set of lessons in this unit will extend our knowledge of trigonometry by finding missing sides and angles of non-right triangles. This lesson will cover the Law of Sines, a law that explores the relationship between the sine of an angle and its opposite side.

 ## Law of Sines Proof

The proof of the Law of Sines starts with an arbitrary triangle shown to the right.

In the triangle, draw an **altitude** which is a perpendicular line drawn through any vertex of the triangle and label it as "h", resembling the "height".

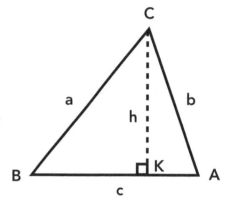

An altitude by definition is perpendicular to the base, so 2 right triangles are created within $\triangle ABC$. Notice that in both $\triangle BCK$ and $\triangle ACK$, the height "h" is shared indicating that the height can be evaluated by using the sine ratios of angles A & B as shown below.

$$\sin(A) = \frac{h}{b} \rightarrow h = b\sin(A)$$

When taking the sine ratio of angles A & B, the height "h" can be simplified as shown. Since both equations are equivalent to the same height, we can set the expressions equal to one another and create the equation below.

$$\sin(B) = \frac{h}{a} \rightarrow h = a\sin(B)$$

$$b\sin(A) = a\sin(B)$$

Use this equation to create a proportion by dividing both sides either by ab or $\sin(A)\sin(B)$.

$$\frac{b\sin(A)}{ab} = \frac{a\sin(B)}{ab} \rightarrow \boxed{\frac{\sin(A)}{a} = \frac{\sin(B)}{b}}$$

or $$\frac{b\sin(A)}{\sin(A)\sin(B)} = \frac{a\sin(B)}{\sin(A)\sin(B)} \rightarrow \boxed{\frac{a}{\sin(A)} = \frac{b}{\sin(B)}}$$

Similarly, if the altitude was drawn through vertex A, it would create the proportion $\dfrac{\sin(B)}{b} = \dfrac{\sin(C)}{c}$.

Since $\dfrac{\sin(A)}{a} = \dfrac{\sin(B)}{b}$, $\dfrac{\sin(A)}{a} = \dfrac{\sin(C)}{c}$ is also true using the Transitive Property of Equality.

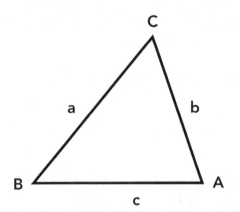

Law of Sines

$$\frac{\sin(A)}{a} = \frac{\sin(B)}{b} = \frac{\sin(C)}{c} \quad \text{or} \quad \frac{a}{\sin(A)} = \frac{b}{\sin(B)} = \frac{c}{\sin(C)}$$

 Example 1   Solve for c in a triangle with A=40°, B=65°, a=5.

Whenever a problem uses the triangle notation covered in lesson 1.2, always start by drawing a triangle illustrating the information given in the problem. Since the sum of all interior angles is 180°, the measurement of angle C can be found to be (180) - (40 + 65) = 75°.

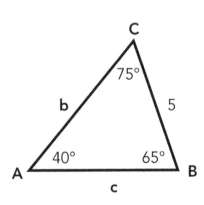

To identify if a problem can utilize the Law of Sines, check if at least one angle has a <u>known</u> measurement and its corresponding side also has a <u>known</u> length.

For example, in the diagram, the measurement of ∠B is known, but the length of side **b** is unknown. However, the measurement of ∠A (40°) and the length of **a** (5 units) is known, so the Law of Sines can be used to solve this problem.

Using the Law of Sines we can deduce the following proportion containing the value we are trying to solve for, i.e. (**c**) and the known measurements of ∠A and side **a**. We can ignore the ratio containing ∠B and side **b** since side **b** is unknown.

$$\frac{\sin(A)}{a} = \frac{\sin(C)}{c} \longrightarrow \frac{\sin(40°)}{5} = \frac{\sin(75°)}{c} \longrightarrow c\sin(40°) = 5\sin(75°)$$

Write the Law of
Sines proportion

Substitute known
values and solve for c

Cross multiply

$$c = \frac{5\sin(75°)}{\sin(40°)} \longrightarrow \boxed{c \approx 7.51}$$

Divide by sin(40°)
on both sides

Calculate the
expression in DEG

 ## Applying to AAS & ASA

As you may have noticed in Example 1, there are only certain instances when the Law of Sines can be applied. This is when there is a known ratio of a side and its corresponding angle. Law of Sines can be used when a triangle has **AAS**, **ASA**, or **SSA**. SSA will be discussed in a later lesson.

AAS or Angle-Angle-Side refers to when two angles and an <u>adjacent</u> side (NOT included) are known and provided. Example 1 is **AAS** since two angles (45° and 65°) and an adjacent side 5 were given in the problem.

ASA or Angle-Side-Angle refers to when two angles and their <u>included</u> side (or side in between two angles) is known. The third angle can be calculated from the two given angles using the Triangle Sum Theorem, and this allows for a sine ratio to be created.

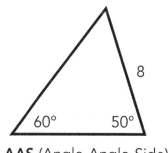

AAS (Angle-Angle-Side)

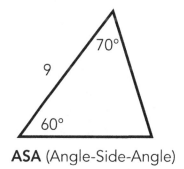

ASA (Angle-Side-Angle)

Some problems may ask you to **solve the triangle**. Simply put in context, solving a triangle is asking you to find <u>all</u> unknown sides and angles of a triangle. For example, if A, C, and b were provided, you must find a, B, and c. Let's solve a triangle using the Law of Sines in example 2 below.

Example 2   **Solve the triangle ABC where C=40°, A=115°, b=9.**

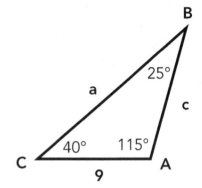

Similar to example 1, always start by drawing a triangle illustrating the information given in the problem. Make sure to label the known <u>and</u> unknown values.
In the diagram, we can identify this scenario as ASA (Angle-Side-Angle) and therefore, the Law of Sines can be used. Finally, using the Triangle Sum Theorem, the measurement of angle B can be found as 25°.

To start, find the unknown value "**a**". We can use the Law of Sines by creating a ratio between the sine of angle B and its corresponding side and set a proportion with the sine of angle A and its unknown side "a".

$$\frac{a}{\sin(A)} = \frac{b}{\sin(B)} \quad \rightarrow \quad \frac{a}{\sin(115°)} = \frac{9}{\sin(25°)} \quad \rightarrow \quad a = \frac{9\sin(115°)}{\sin(25°)} \quad \rightarrow \quad \boxed{a \approx 19.3}$$

Write the Law of   Substitute known   Multiply by sin(115°)
Sines proportion   values and solve for a   on both sides

Similarly, to find the unknown value "**c**", we can use the Law of Sines by creating a proportion between the sine of angle B & side "b" and the sine of angle C & corresponding unknown side "c".

$$\frac{c}{\sin(C)} = \frac{b}{\sin(B)} \quad \rightarrow \quad \frac{c}{\sin(40°)} = \frac{9}{\sin(25°)} \quad \rightarrow \quad c = \frac{9\sin(40°)}{\sin(25°)} \quad \rightarrow \quad \boxed{c \approx 13.69}$$

Write the Law of   Substitute known   Multiply by sin(40°) on
Sines proportion   values and solve for c   both sides

As our final answer, here are the values of all the angles A, B, C, and sides a, b, c of triangle ABC as shown below:

A = 115°   a = 19.3

B = 25°   b = 9

C = 40°   c = 13.69

5.2 Practice Problems

Solve the triangle ABC in each of following problems.

1   A=25°, a=7, B=69°

2   B=34°, C=120°, a=11

3   A=48°, a=7, C=86°

4   A=92°, b=16, C=56°

5   B=45°, A=60°, c=10

6   C=77°, c=14, B=33°

5.3 The Ambiguous Case

In the previous lesson, you learned about the Law of Sines and how it can be applied to find missing sides of ASA & AAS triangles. In this lesson, we will learn about the ambiguous case, also known as SSA, which requires more analysis before the Law of Sines can be applied.

SSA or Side-Side-Angle refers to when two sides and their <u>adjacent</u> angle (NOT included) are provided in a problem.

 ## Obtuse Cases

Below are obtuse triangles with a <u>fixed</u> obtuse angle "A" and <u>fixed</u> adjacent side "b" that **cannot** change length. We will be exploring how changing the length of side "a" affects the possible triangles.

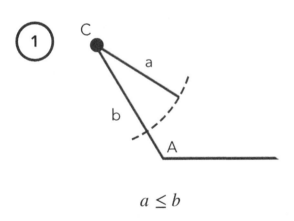

$$a \leq b$$

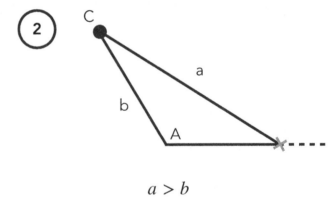

$$a > b$$

If vertex C is treated as a pivot point, then when side "a" is rotated, it is not long enough to intersect at any portion of the base. Therefore, if a ≤ b, **no triangle is possible** and the Law of Sines will not work.

If vertex C is treated as a pivot point, then when side "a" is rotated, it is long enough to intersect at the base and form a triangle. Therefore, if a > b, **one triangle is possible** and the Law of Sines would work.

⚙ Acute Cases

Similar to the obtuse cases, below are acute triangles with a <u>fixed</u> acute angle "A", <u>fixed</u> adjacent side "b", and a <u>fixed</u> perpendicular height "h" that **cannot** change length. Notice how changing the length of side "a" affects the possible triangles.

①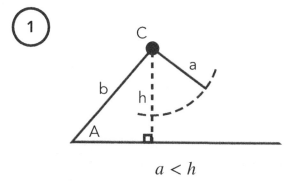

$$a < h$$

If vertex C is treated as a pivot point, the side "a" when rotated is not long enough to intersect any portion of the base. Therefore, if a < h, **no triangle is possible** and the Law of Sines will not work.

②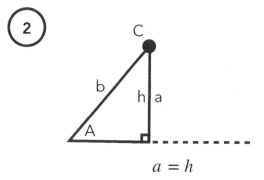

$$a = h$$

The side "a" when rotated is exactly long enough to intersect the base at a right angle and is equivalent to the height. Therefore, if a = h, **one right triangle is possible**.

③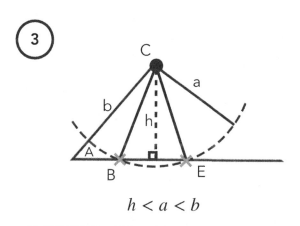

$$h < a < b$$

When side "a" rotates, since it is between the length of "h" and "b", it crosses the base at two points creating △ACB & △ACE.
Therefore, if h < a < b and the side lengths "b", "a", and angle A are known, **two triangles are possible** and the Law of Sines will produce two results.

④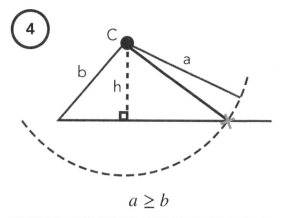

$$a \geq b$$

Since side "a" is longer than "b", "a" will only cross the base at one point before extending away from the triangle and not intersecting the base again.
Therefore, if a ≥ b, **one triangle is possible** and the Law of Sines will produce a single result.

To reinforce, the ambiguous cases shown above illustrate how many possible triangles can exist with two given sides and a non-included angle. Let's now explore how to apply these cases in the examples below.

Example 1   Find the angle C in $\triangle ABC$ where B=35°, b=6, c=9.

First, always make sure to sketch out the entire triangle ABC labeled with your known information. Although we do not know if side "b" will intersect the base, for now, let's assume it does.

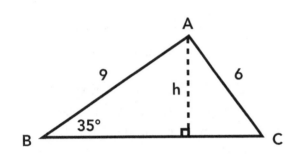

The problem provided only an acute angle, so we only need to analyze the <u>acute</u> cases. In most of the instances, you may notice that the pivoting side (in this case, side "b") and the perpendicular height are compared. So, let's first find the perpendicular height "h".

$$\sin(35°) = \frac{h}{9} \longrightarrow h = 9\sin(35°) \longrightarrow h \approx 5.16$$

Setup the sine ratio   Multiply by 9 on both sides   Evaluate

Looking at the height, we see that the measure of the side length "b", which is 6, is in between the length of height "h" and side "c". Therefore, since h < b < c, this matches Acute Case 3 on the previous page and **2 triangles are possible**.

To find the measure of angle C for one of the possible triangle, use the Law of Sines by creating a proportion of side b, angle B, side c, and the unknown angle C.

$$\frac{\sin(C)}{c} = \frac{\sin(B)}{b} \longrightarrow \frac{\sin(C)}{9} = \frac{\sin(35°)}{6} \longrightarrow \sin(C) = \frac{9\sin(35°)}{6}$$

Write the Law of Sines proportion   Substitute known values and solve for C   Multiply by 9 on both sides

Remember, to solve for C, we will need to apply inverse trigonometry learned in lesson 2.4 by taking the inverse sine of the ratio in order to find the measure of its degree C.
Using the domain of inverse sine covered in lesson 5.1, the following expression will only result in a positive acute angle.

$$C = \sin^{-1}\left(\frac{9\sin(35°)}{6} \right) \longrightarrow \boxed{C \approx 59.36°} \qquad \textbf{Triangle 1}$$

Take the sine inverse   Evaluate in DEG mode

However, in order to identify the second triangle that can be formed, we still need to find the second value of angle C. To find this second angle, we can pivot side "b" on point A and see how it will intersect the base & create a new triangle $\triangle ABC'$ (referred to as "ABC prime").

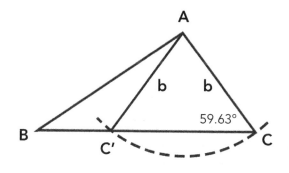

When side b is pivoted, it intersects the base at the point C' (C prime). If we look at the triangle $\triangle ACC'$, two sides have the length "b" and this makes the triangle isosceles.

As per the Base Angle Theorem, the angles across the congruent sides are also congruent. So, this means $m\angle AC'C = 59.63°$.
If we are trying to find the angle of C' ($\angle AC'B$) of the second triangle, notice how $\angle AC'C$ and $\angle AC'B$ are linear pairs. This means that they are supplementary angles, so the sum of the angles are 180°.

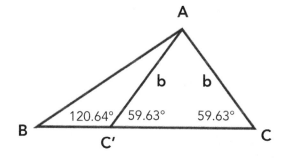

$m\angle AC'B = 180° - 59.63° = 120.64°$, so the second triangle has C = 120.64°.

$$\boxed{C' \approx 120.64°} \qquad \textbf{Triangle 2}$$

Note that whenever you create the second triangle for Acute Case 3, always label the angles and sides with a PRIME symbol ('). For example, A = 85.37° but A' = 24.36°.

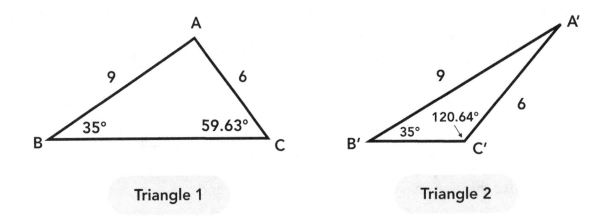

Triangle 1

Triangle 2

Example 2

Find the angle B in $\triangle ABC$ where C=21°, b=11, c=3.

As always, make sure to draw out the entire triangle ABC labeled with all the known information.

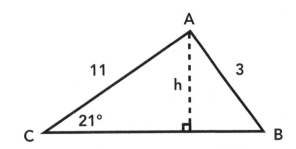

In this problem, we are once again provided with an acute angle and need to find the perpendicular height "h" to compare with side "c".

$$\sin(21°) = \frac{h}{11} \;\longrightarrow\; h = 11\sin(21°) \;\longrightarrow\; h \approx 3.94$$

Setup the sine ratio

Multiply by 11 on both sides

Evaluate

Looking at the height, we see that the measure of the side length "c" = 3, is slightly less than the length of the height "h" ~ 3.94. Therefore, since c < h, this matches Acute Case 1 and **no triangle can be formed.** Based upon this evaluation, <u>this problem cannot be solved.</u>

5.3 Practice Problems

Solve the triangle ABC in each of the following problems.

1 C=121°, c=16, a=10

2 B=49°, c=9, b=8

3 a=8, A=75°, b=11

4 A=80°, c=20, a=24

5 C=53°, b=10, c=8.5

6 B=29°, b=17, a=14

7 A=99°, b=25, a=19

8 C=30°, c=9, b=18

5.4 Law of Cosines

In the previous two lessons, we have learned the Law of Sines and its applications in ASA, AAS, SSA triangles. Now we will learn a new law called the Law of Cosines which can be applied to other non-right triangles such as SAS and SSS.

 ## Law of Cosines Proof

To begin the proof of the Law of Cosines, let's use the same arbitrary triangle we defined for the Law of Sines Proof. Except, let's split segment "c" into two segments: the right segment as "d" and the other segment as "c-d" as per the Segment Addition Postulate.

First, we notice two inner triangles $\triangle AKC$ & $\triangle BKC$ inside the large triangle $\triangle ABC$. Let's use the Pythagorean theorem on each of these inner triangles to have some equations to work with.

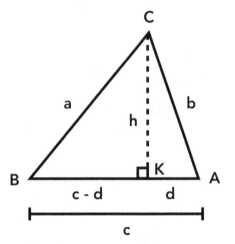

$$a^2 = h^2 + (c-d)^2$$

$$b^2 = h^2 + d^2$$

$$h^2 = b^2 - d^2$$

$$\cos(A) = \frac{b}{d} \longrightarrow d = b\cos(A) \longrightarrow h^2 = b^2 - (b\cos(A))^2$$

In the triangle towards right, "d" can also be defined as simply $d = b\cos(A)$ from the ratio $\cos(A) = \frac{b}{d}$. We can then use systems of equations to combine both of these equations together and remove the variable h^2.

$$a^2 = h^2 + (c-d)^2 \longrightarrow a^2 = b^2 - (b\cos(A))^2 + (c - b\cos(A))^2$$

$$\longrightarrow a^2 = b^2 - b^2\cos(A)^2 + c^2 - 2cb\cos(A) + b^2\cos(A)^2$$

$$\longrightarrow \boxed{a^2 = b^2 + c^2 - 2bc\cos(A)}$$

If the height was drawn through vertices A or B, then the equations shown below could also be derived using the same process. These equations are known as the Law of Cosines.

Law of Cosines

$$a^2 = b^2 + c^2 - 2bc \cos A$$

$$b^2 = a^2 + c^2 - 2ac \cos B$$

$$c^2 = a^2 + b^2 - 2ab \cos C$$

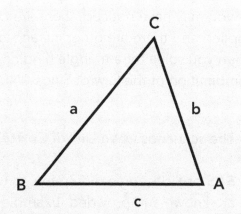

Similar to the Law of Sines, the Law of Cosines can also be used to solve for missing sides and angles as shown in example 1 below.

🔍 **Example 1**   **Find the side a in $\triangle ABC$ where A=48°, b=5, c=9.**

As always, make sure to draw out the entire triangle ABC labeled with all the known information.

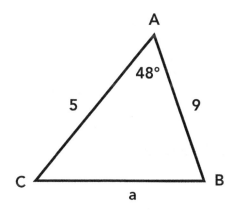

In the diagram, we notice that the opposite side of angle A (side a) is missing. However, since we are given the measurement of angle A, we can use the first Law of Cosines equation and substitute the known values to solve for side "a".

$$a^2 = b^2 + c^2 - 2bc \cos A$$

$$a^2 = 5^2 + 9^2 - 2(5)(9)\cos(48°)$$

$$a^2 \approx 45.78$$

$$\boxed{a \approx 6.77}$$

Applying to SAS & SSS

As you may have noticed, there are certain instances when the Law of Cosines can be applied and there are other instances when only the Law of Sines can be used. Sometimes, when you solve for a triangle (finding ALL missing angles and sides), you may need to use a combination of the Law of Sines AND the Law of Cosines.

The scenarios when Law of Cosines can be used are **SAS & SSS.**

SAS or Side-Angle-Side refers to when two sides and their <u>included</u> side (in between) are known and provided. Example 1 is **SAS** since the included angle (48°) and its two adjacent sides 5 & 9 were given in the problem.

SSS or Side-Side-Side refers to when ALL sides are known and provided by the problem. This allows any of the Law of Cosines equations to be applied in such a problem since all sides are given and any one angle can be solved.

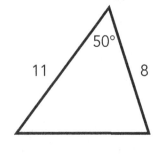

SAS (Side-Angle-Side)

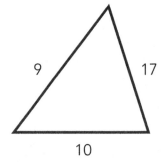

SSS (Side-Side-Side)

The table below summarizes when the Law of Sines & Cosines are used.

NOTE

Law of Sines	AAS	ASA	SSA
Law of Cosines	SAS	SSS	

Example 2   **Solve the triangle $\triangle ABC$ where a=6, b=12, c=16.**

As always, make sure to draw out the entire triangle ABC labeled with all the known information.

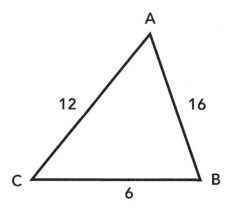

In the diagram, we are provided all of the sides and need to find the interior angles A, B, and C. This is classified as a **SSS Case** and we can use the Law of Cosines. To start, let's find the measure of angle B by using the second Law of Cosines equation.

$$b^2 = a^2 + c^2 - 2ac\cos B$$

$$12^2 = 6^2 + 16^2 - 2(6)(16)\cos B$$

$$144 = 292 - 192\cos B \longrightarrow \cos B = \frac{148}{192} \longrightarrow B = \arccos\left(\frac{148}{192}\right)$$

Simplify

Form cosine ratio

Take the inverse to find the degree

$$\boxed{B = 39.57°}$$

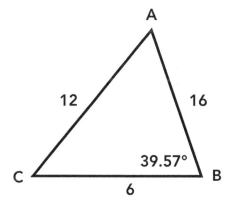

Since we now have the measure of one of the angles, we have a pair of a <u>known</u> angle and a <u>known</u> side, so the **Law of Sines** can be applied.

In order to find the measure of angle C, set up a proportion between angle B and side b with angle C and side c.

$$\frac{\sin C}{c} = \frac{\sin B}{b} \longrightarrow \frac{\sin C}{16} = \frac{\sin 39.57°}{12}$$

$$\sin C = \frac{16\sin 39.57°}{12}$$

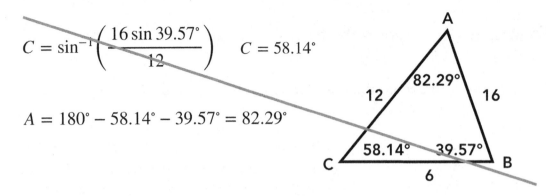

$$C = \sin^{-1}\left(\frac{16\sin 39.57°}{12}\right) \qquad C = 58.14°$$

$$A = 180° - 58.14° - 39.57° = 82.29°$$

Our instinct is to take the inverse sine of the ratio to find the measure of angle C. However, in any triangle, **the longest side ALWAYS corresponds to the biggest angle**. But, the biggest angle in this situation is corresponding to the shortest side. This means that these angle measures are incorrect.

This is because the following triangle is actually OBTUSE, with C being the obtuse angle. As per the unit circle, it is possible to have an acute angle and an obtuse angle sharing the same sine, but different cosines.

Since sine inverse only has a domain between $-90° \le \theta \le 90°$, your calculator will **never** output an obtuse angle. Therefore, in order to identify if a triangle has an obtuse angle, **always perform the Law of Cosines on the biggest angle first (SSS only) and THEN use the Law of Sines OR Cosines.** This is because cosine inverse can output an acute OR an obtuse angle (domain: $0° \le \theta \le 180°$). To identify the biggest angle, **find the angle opposite to the longest side** first.

Let's rework this problem by using the Law of Cosines on the biggest angle C **first** since it is across the longest side (16). We will use the third equation of the Law of Cosines.

$$c^2 = a^2 + b^2 - 2ab\cos C \quad \longrightarrow \quad 16^2 = 6^2 + 12^2 - 2(6)(12)\cos C$$

$$\cos C = -\frac{76}{144} \quad \longrightarrow \quad C = \arccos\left(-\frac{76}{144}\right) \quad \longrightarrow \quad \boxed{C = 121.86°}$$

The angle measure for C is way bigger than before! Assuming measure of angle B remains the same since the Law of Cosines was used, find the measure of angle A using Triangle Sum.

$$A = 180° - 121.86° - 39.57° = 18.57°$$

A = 18.57° B = 39.57° C = 121.86°

5.4 Practice Problems

Solve the triangle ABC for each of the following problems.

1 a=9, b=10, c=11

2 c=14, b=8, a=9

3 a=10, B=78°, c=19

4 C=32°, a=16, b=17

5 b=7, c=15, a=10

6 A=137°, b=21, c=5

7 B=49°, b=19, c=23

8 a=11, b=6, c=6

116

Unit

6

Trigonometric Identities

6.1 Introduction to Identities

Welcome to a new unit on identities! In this unit, we will be using our knowledge of the unit circle and algebra to derive trigonometric identities and formulas that can be applied in numerous problems. A **trigonometric identity** is an equation which simplifies an expression and is true for any value of θ. In fact, we have already learned some basic identities in the previous chapters.

> Note: Located in A.3 of the appendix is a trigonometric identities sheet which can be used as a reference throughout this chapter.

 ## Reciprocal & Quotient Identities

Let's review some basic identities first. As per our definitions of trigonometric ratios, the reciprocal identities are the same as the 3 additional ratios we learned in lesson 2.5. These are the cosecant, secant, and cotangent ratios referenced below as well.

Reciprocal Identities

$$\csc \theta = \frac{1}{\sin \theta} \qquad \sec \theta = \frac{1}{\cos \theta} \qquad \cot \theta = \frac{1}{\tan \theta}$$

Using the unit circle diagram as our reference and knowing that x is $\cos \theta$ and y is $\sin \theta$, we can conclude that the tangent and cotangent of the angle will result in the following quotient identities:

Quotient Identities

$$\tan \theta = \frac{\sin \theta}{\cos \theta} \qquad \cot \theta = \frac{\cos \theta}{\sin \theta}$$

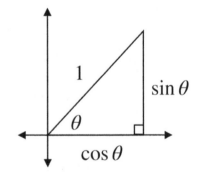

Pythagorean Identities

Let's now take a closer look at the unit circle diagram labeled with sine and cosine as the legs. Since this is a right triangle, we can use the Pythagorean Theorem, i.e. the sum of square of each leg is equal to the square of hypotenuse (which is just 1).
This identity is very crucial and once again, applies to ANY angle.

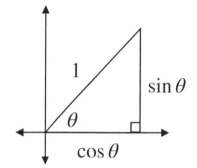

$$\sin^2 \theta + \cos^2 \theta = 1$$

We can create 2 more Pythagorean Identities solely from this equation.
For the second identity, divide by $\sin^2 \theta$ on both sides and simplify the ratio.
For the third identity, divide by $\cos^2 \theta$ from both sides and simplify the ratio.

Note: When multiple squared trigonometric ratios are dividing one another, it is simply the entire expression squared as shown below.

① $\quad \dfrac{\sin^2 \theta}{\sin^2 \theta} + \dfrac{\cos^2 \theta}{\sin^2 \theta} = \dfrac{1}{\sin^2 \theta} \quad \longrightarrow \quad 1 + \underbrace{\left(\dfrac{\cos \theta}{\sin \theta}\right)^2}_{\substack{\text{Quotient}\\\text{Identity}}} = \underbrace{\left(\dfrac{1}{\sin \theta}\right)^2}_{\substack{\text{Reciprocal}\\\text{Identity}}}$

$$1 + \cot^2 \theta = \csc^2 \theta$$

② $\quad \dfrac{\sin^2 \theta}{\cos^2 \theta} + \dfrac{\cos^2 \theta}{\cos^2 \theta} = \dfrac{1}{\cos^2 \theta} \quad \longrightarrow \quad \underbrace{\left(\dfrac{\sin \theta}{\cos \theta}\right)^2}_{\substack{\text{Quotient}\\\text{Identity}}} + 1 = \underbrace{\left(\dfrac{1}{\cos \theta}\right)^2}_{\substack{\text{Reciprocal}\\\text{Identity}}}$

$$\tan^2 \theta + 1 = \sec^2 \theta$$

Cofunction Identities

When creating a triangle on the unit circle, we usually focus on the angle θ between the initial and terminal side. However, since this is a right triangle, there are two acute angles that exist. Since they must add up to $\frac{\pi}{2}$ rad, the other angle must be $\frac{\pi}{2} - \theta$ rad.

By performing trigonometric ratios on this new angle, we can create the **cofunction** identities.

For example, $\tan\left(\frac{\pi}{2} - \theta\right)$ is the ratio of the opposite side from $(\frac{\pi}{2} - \theta)$ over the adjacent side near $(\frac{\pi}{2} - \theta)$. In other words, which is basically $\cos\theta$ (opposite side) over $\sin\theta$ (adjacent side), resulting in $\cot\theta$.

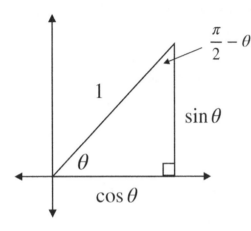

Cofunction Identities

$$\sin\left(\frac{\pi}{2} - \theta\right) = \cos\theta \quad \csc\left(\frac{\pi}{2} - \theta\right) = \sec\theta$$

$$\cos\left(\frac{\pi}{2} - \theta\right) = \sin\theta \quad \sec\left(\frac{\pi}{2} - \theta\right) = \csc\theta$$

$$\tan\left(\frac{\pi}{2} - \theta\right) = \cot\theta \quad \cot\left(\frac{\pi}{2} - \theta\right) = \tan\theta$$

 # Even & Odd Identities

In the diagram to the right, we focus on examining what happens when the angle θ is negated. The x-value remains the same ($\cos\theta$) since the bases are shared, but the y-value ($\sin\theta$) is flipped and thus negative. Using trigonometric ratios on the angle $-\theta$, we can create the **even & odd identities**.

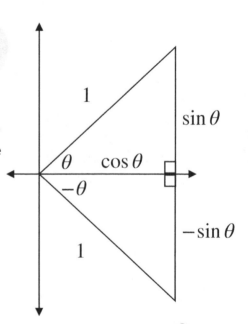

For example, $\cot(-\theta)$ is the ratio of the adjacent side from $-\theta$ (which is $\cos\theta$) over the opposite side (which is $-\sin\theta$), resulting in $-\cot\theta$.

Even & Odd Identities

$$\sin(-\theta) = -\sin\theta \qquad \cos(-\theta) = \cos\theta \qquad \tan(-\theta) = -\tan\theta$$

$$\csc(-\theta) = -\csc\theta \qquad \sec(-\theta) = \sec\theta \qquad \cot(-\theta) = -\cot\theta$$

Q Example 1

If $\sec(72°) = 3.24$, **find a)** $\tan(72°)$ **and b)** $\cot(-18°)$ **using trigonometric identities.**

a Given the secant of 72°, we can find the tangent of that angle by using the third Pythagorean identity. We can set $\theta = 72°$ and solve for $\tan\theta$.

$$\tan^2\theta + 1 = \sec^2\theta \longrightarrow \tan^2(72°) + 1 = \sec^2(72°) \longrightarrow \tan^2(72°) = 3.24^2 - 1$$

Setup identity   Substitute angle   Simplify

$$\tan(72°) = \sqrt{9.4976} \longrightarrow \tan(72°) = 3.08$$

Take positive square root since angle
is in Q1 and tangent is positive

b Once we find $\tan(72°) = 3.08$, we can use a cofunction identity to find $\cot 18°$. Then, we can use an odd identity to find $\cot(-18°)$.

$$\tan(90° - \theta) = \cot\theta \longrightarrow \tan(90° - 18°) = \cot 18° \longrightarrow \cot 18° = 3.08$$

Setup identity formatted
with degrees, not radians

Substitute θ for 18° so the left
side can simplify to $\tan(72°)$

$$\cot(-\theta) = -\cot(\theta) \longrightarrow \cot(-18°) = -\cot(18°) \longrightarrow \cot(-18°) = -3.08$$

Setup the odd identity

Substitue θ for 18°

Q Example 2 Simplify $(1 - \sin\theta)^2(1 + 2\tan\theta\cos\theta + \csc\theta\sin^3\theta)$

This expression may seem quite complicated, but whenever simplifying a trigonometric expression, there are 5 key things you want to usually look out for:

1. Always apply the reciprocal and quotient identities whenever possible.

2. If fractions are involved, simplify by finding common denominators.

3. Use Pythagorean Identities whenever possible (especially look out for trigonometric functions that are squared). If there is a fraction, try to multiply the numerator and denominator with an expression that creates a Pythagorean Identity.

4. Factor and use difference of squares whenever possible (multiplying by conjugate).

5. Always have everything in terms of positive θ unless otherwise stated (i.e. not $(-\theta)$, $(\pi/2 - \theta)$, etc.)

To start simplifying this expression, let's look at the embedded expression in the second set of parentheses. As mentioned in the above tips:

First apply the reciprocal identity to cosecant terms and apply the quotient identity to the tangent terms. This cancels a $\cos(\theta)$ in the second term, leaving just $\sin\theta$, and cancels a $\sin\theta$ in the third term, leaving $\sin^2\theta$ using properties of exponents.

$$1 + 2\tan\theta\cos\theta + \csc\theta\sin^3\theta \longrightarrow 1 + 2\frac{\sin\theta}{\cos\theta}\cdot\cos\theta + \frac{1}{\sin\theta}\cdot\sin^3\theta$$

$$1 + 2\sin\theta + \sin^2\theta$$

This embedded expression can also be factored similar to a quadratic function. However, we would need to use u-substitution such that $u = \sin\theta$ and this temporary variable "u" can be in place of $\sin\theta$. Then factor as normal in terms of u, and substitute u back for $\sin\theta$ to have the factored expression $(1 + \sin\theta)^2$.

122

$$1 + 2\sin\theta + \sin^2\theta \longrightarrow 1 + 2u + u^2 \longrightarrow (1+u)^2 \longrightarrow (1+\sin\theta)^2$$

Substitute $\sin\theta$ with u Factor perfect binomial   Substitute u back for $\sin\theta$

We have now created a simple expression in terms of binomials: $(1 - \sin\theta)^2(1 + \sin\theta)^2$. However, this can be simplified even further. Since two multiplying factors are being raised to the same exponent, 2, the entire expression can be squared: $[(1 - \sin\theta)(1 + \sin\theta)]^2$.

Since these factors are conjugates, the inner expression is a difference of squares and can be expanded as shown below. Notice how the sine ratio is squared and there is a 1. This means that the first Pythagorean Identity can be used and if this identity is rewritten by subtracting $\sin^2\theta$ from both sides. Therefore, $\cos^2\theta$ can be substituted and the expression can be written as $\cos^4\theta$ in its simplest form.

$$[(1 - \sin\theta)(1 + \sin\theta)]^2 \longrightarrow (1 - \sin^2\theta)^2$$

$$\sin^2\theta + \cos^2\theta = 1$$

$$\longrightarrow (\cos^2\theta)^2 \longrightarrow \cos^4\theta$$

$$\cos^2\theta = 1 - \sin^2\theta$$

6.1 Practice Problems

For #1-3, find the trigonometric ratios (a),(b),(c) based on the given ratio in each problem <u>without</u> using a calculator.

1 $\cos\left(\dfrac{\pi}{11}\right) = 0.9595$

   a) $\sin\left(\dfrac{\pi}{11}\right)$

   b) $\cot\left(\dfrac{9\pi}{22}\right)$

   c) $\tan\left(-\dfrac{9\pi}{22}\right)$

2 $\sin\left(\dfrac{5\pi}{7}\right) = 0.782$

   a) $\tan\left(\dfrac{5\pi}{7}\right)$

   b) $\cos\left(\dfrac{3\pi}{14}\right)$

   c) $\sec\left(\dfrac{2\pi}{7}\right)$

3 $\csc\phi = \dfrac{5}{a}$

   $0 < \phi < \dfrac{\pi}{2}$

   a) $\sin\left(\dfrac{\pi}{2} - \phi\right)$

   b) $\cot\phi$

   c) $-\csc(\pi - \phi)$

For #4-9, simplify or condense the trigonometric expression as much as possible.

4 $\csc\theta - \cos\theta\cot\theta$

5 $\dfrac{\tan\theta\sec\theta}{\sin\theta} - \tan^2\theta$

6 $\sin\beta(\tan\beta\csc^2\beta - 1)(\sec\beta)$

7 $(\sec\theta - \sin\theta\tan\theta)^{-2} - 1$

8 $\dfrac{\sec^2\left(\frac{\pi}{2} - x\right)}{\csc^2 x + \tan^2 x - \sec^2 x} - 1$

9 $\dfrac{\sin\theta}{1 - \cos\theta} + \dfrac{1 - \cos\theta}{\sin\theta}$

6.2 Verifying Identities

This lesson will expand upon the identities learned in lesson 6.1. So far we learned how to simplify trigonometric expressions using the basic identities. Now we will try to **verify** these identities with other trigonometric expressions.

 ## How to Verify Identities

A verifying identity problem asks you to **prove** how 2 different trigonometric expressions are equivalent to one another (ex. $1 - \cos^2\theta = \csc^{-2}\theta$).

In an identity proof, we can **only simplify and condense one side of the equation (either the left or right side).** If we modify the expressions on both sides, we are assuming that both expressions are equivalent, which is an assumption we cannot make.

Since this is a proof, it must be done in a proper mathematical format. In this unit, we will be using the **Statements** & **Reasons** structure as shown below. On the left side are the statements, where we show our mathematical simplification work of each step. And on the right side, we write down what specific step was performed to simplify the expression.

Finally, to formally end a proof, we write Q.E.D. (a latin abbreviation meaning "which has been demonstrated") and/or a small square on the very bottom of the proof.

Statements	Reasons	
$1 - \cos^2\theta = \csc^{-2}\theta$	Given	When formatting a proof, make sure to start with the equation you are going to prove called the "given" statement.
$= \dfrac{1}{\csc^2\theta}$	Negative Exponents	Then, simplify one side of the expression and either rewrite the other side in every step or draw an arrow to show repetition till the very final step.
$= \sin^2\theta$	Reciprocal Identity	
$1 - \cos^2\theta = 1 - \cos^2\theta$	Pythagorean Identity	For each simplification, write the reason used to simplify such as the definition of negative exponents, combining like terms, finding common denominators, and other trigonometric identities.
	∎ Q.E.D.	

125

Example 1   Verify $\dfrac{\cot x}{\csc x - 1} + \dfrac{\csc x - 1}{\cot x} = 2\sec x$

Before we start proving the above equation, lets first identify which <u>side</u> to simplify. **Always select the one that looks more complex (e.g. with many components or values) to simplify.** This is because proving the more complex side is actually much easier than solving the lesser complicated one. Therefore, we will start by simplifying the left side which seems more complex.

Statements	**Reasons**
$\dfrac{\cot x}{\csc x - 1} + \dfrac{\csc x - 1}{\cot x} = 2\sec x$	Given
$\dfrac{\cot x}{\csc x - 1}\left(\dfrac{\cot x}{\cot x}\right) + \dfrac{\csc x - 1}{\cot x}\left(\dfrac{\csc x - 1}{\csc x - 1}\right) =$	Common Denominators

Since these are complex fractions, multiply the numerator and denominator of the first and second fraction by $\cot x$ and $\csc x - 1$ respectively to form common denominators so the fractions can be added together. Then, the first fraction can be simplified with exponents and since the second fraction is a binomial squared, it can be expanded using binomial expansion. Both of these reasons can be combined into the same step.

| $\dfrac{\boxed{\cot^2 x} + \csc^2 x - 2\csc x + \boxed{1}}{(\cot x)(\csc x - 1)} =$ | Simplify & Binomial Expansion |

The Pythagorean Identity $1 + \cot^2 x = \csc^2 x$ can be used to combine the circled terms and simplify the numerator as shown below.

| $\dfrac{2\csc^2 x - 2\csc x}{(\cot x)(\csc x - 1)} =$ | Pythagorean Identity & Combine Like Terms |

| Common terms indicate to factor and simplify! | $\dfrac{2\csc x(\csc x - 1)}{(\cot x)(\csc x - 1)} =$ | Factor Common Factor & Simplify |

$$2 \csc x \tan x =$$

Reciprocal Identity

$$2\left(\frac{1}{\cancel{\sin x}}\right)\left(\frac{\cancel{\sin x}}{\cos x}\right) =$$

Reciprocal Identity &
Quotient Identity

$$2 \sec x = 2 \sec x$$

Simplify & Reciprocal
Identity

■ Q.E.D.

Thankfully, with the proofs, it is easier to know if you are solving it in a right way as when you are trying to solve one side to the equation and you are able to arrive at the same expression as the other side (opposite to the equal sign).

Q   **Example 2**   **Verify** $(\cot \theta + \tan \theta)^2 = \csc^2 \theta \sec^2 \theta$.

For this problem, let's simplify the left side of this equation since these terms can be easily expanded and simplified using identities. Set up the proof with the statements and reasons structure as shown below.

Statements	Reasons
$(\cot \theta + \tan \theta)^2 = \csc^2 \theta \sec^2 \theta$	Given
$\left(\dfrac{\cos \theta}{\sin \theta} + \dfrac{\sin \theta}{\cos \theta}\right)^2 =$	Reciprocal Identity

Although we could have expanded the entire binomial, the reciprocal identities within the squared expression are easier to simplify as shown in the steps below.

Now since there are two fractions being added in the expression, we must use the common denominator $\sin\theta\cos\theta$ to combine both fractions together.

When the fractions are combined, the Pythagorean Identity $\sin^2\theta + \cos^2\theta = 1$ can be used to simplify the numerator.

$$\left[\frac{\cos\theta}{\sin\theta}\left(\frac{\cos\theta}{\cos\theta}\right) + \frac{\sin\theta}{\cos\theta}\left(\frac{\sin\theta}{\sin\theta}\right)\right]^2 = \qquad \text{Common Denominators}$$

$$\left(\frac{\sin^2\theta + \cos^2\theta}{\sin\theta\cos\theta}\right)^2 = \qquad \text{Simplify}$$

$$\left(\frac{1}{\sin\theta\cos\theta}\right)^2 = \qquad \text{Pythagorean Identity}$$

Now, the exponent can be distributed to the numerator term (which remains 1) and the denominator terms (which become $\sin^2\theta\cos^2\theta$). Finally, the fraction can be split into two factors and rewritten in terms of their reciprocal trigonometric ratios as shown below.

$$\frac{1}{\sin^2\theta\cos^2\theta} = \qquad \text{Exponent Property}$$

$$\left(\frac{1}{\sin\theta}\right)^2 \cdot \left(\frac{1}{\cos\theta}\right)^2 = \qquad \text{Rewriting expression}$$

$$\csc^2\theta\sec^2\theta = \csc^2\theta\sec^2\theta \qquad \text{Reciprocal Identity}$$

■ Q.E.D.

6.2 Practice Problems

For #1-10, verify the trigonometric identity for each of the following problems.

1 $\dfrac{1 - \sin x}{\cos x} + \dfrac{\cos x}{1 + \sin x} = \dfrac{2 \cos x}{1 + \sin x}$

2 $\sec \theta + \tan \theta = \dfrac{\cos \theta}{1 - \sin \theta}$

3 $\cos \alpha \cot \alpha + \sin \alpha - \csc \alpha = 0$

4 $\sin(-x) = \dfrac{\sin^2 x - 1}{\csc x - \tan x \cos x}$

5 $(\tan x + 1)^2 (\cot x + 1)^2 = (\sec x \csc x + 2)^2$

6 $\dfrac{\csc \beta}{\tan \beta + \cot \beta} = \cos \beta$

7 $\dfrac{\tan x}{1 + \sec x} - \dfrac{1 + \sec x}{\tan x} = -2 \cot x$

8 $\dfrac{\cos x \cot x}{\csc x - 1} = 1 + \sin x$

9 $\tan^4 x + \tan^2 x = \sec^4 x - \sec^2 x$

10 $\sqrt{\dfrac{\csc \theta + 1}{\csc \theta - 1}} = \dfrac{\cos \theta}{1 - \sin \theta}$

After understanding basic identities in lesson 6.1, lets now learn a new set of identities called the sum and difference identities. These identities involve finding the trigonometric ratio of an angle (such as 15°) by splitting them into the sum or difference of two separate angles (45° - 30°). The following is a sample proof explaining the derivation of these identities.

 ## Sum & Difference Identities Proof

To start, consider two rays and two radii on the unit circle forming angles **a** and **b** as shown. The angle formed between the two rays is the angle measure **a-b**. Per the definition of unit circle, the coordinates $(\cos a, \sin a)$ and $(\cos b, \sin b)$ are defined as the points where the terminal side of each angle intersects the unit circle, based on the sine and cosine values.

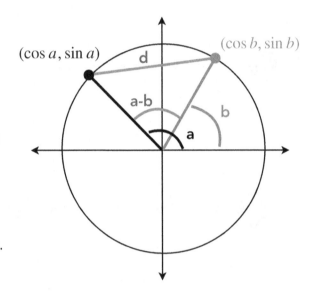

Let's find the length **d** between the segments using the distance formula on these coordinates.

$$d = \sqrt{(\cos a - \cos b)^2 + (\sin a - \sin b)^2}$$

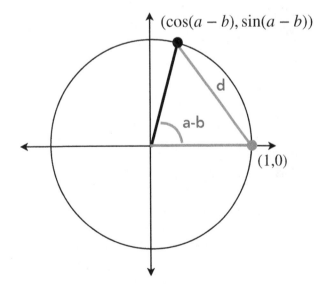

Suppose the rays are rotated while maintaining the same angles as shown in the diagram to the left. When isolating only angle (**a-b**), the point intersected by the terminal side can be written in terms of the cosine and sine of (**a-b**) as per the unit circle definition.

The distance formula can then be used once again to write another expression for **d**.

$$d = \sqrt{(\cos(a - b) - 1)^2 + (\sin(a - b) - 0)^2}$$

Since the length of **d** has been defined as two different expressions, we will set both expressions equal to one another and solve for $\cos(a - b)$ to find the cosine difference identity. Remember that f(a-b) ≠ f(a) - f(b), so $\cos(a - b) \neq \cos(a) - \cos(b)$.

$$\sqrt{(\cos a - \cos b)^2 + (\sin a - \sin b)^2} = \sqrt{(\cos(a - b) - 1)^2 + (\sin(a - b) - 0)^2}$$

$$(\cos a - \cos b)^2 + (\sin a - \sin b)^2 = (\cos(a - b) - 1)^2 + \sin^2(a - b)$$

$$\cos^2 a - 2\cos a \cos b + \cos^2 b + \sin^2 a - 2\sin a \sin b + \sin^2 b$$
$$= \cos^2(a - b) - 2\cos(a - b) + 1 + \sin^2(a - b)$$

$$(\sin^2 a + \cos^2 a) + (\sin^2 b + \cos^2 b) - 2(\cos a \cos b + \sin a \sin b)$$
$$= (\sin^2(a - b) + \cos^2(a - b)) + 1 - 2\cos(a - b)$$

$$\cancel{2} - \cancel{2}(\cos a \cos b + \sin a \sin b) = \cancel{2} - \cancel{2}\cos(a - b)$$

$$\boxed{\cos(a - b) = \cos a \cos b + \sin a \sin b}$$

Yay, we found the cosine difference identity! To find the cosine sum identity, substitute **b** for **-b** and apply the even & odd identities.

$$\cos(a - (-b)) = \cos a \cos(-b) + \sin a \sin(-b)$$

$$\boxed{\cos(a + b) = \cos a \cos b - \sin a \sin b}$$

To find the sine sum and difference identities, write out the cofunction identity as:
$\sin \theta = \cos\left(\dfrac{\pi}{2} - \theta\right)$ but substitute θ for **a+b** and evaluate.

$$\sin(a + b) = \cos\left(\frac{\pi}{2} - (a + b)\right) \longrightarrow \sin(a + b) = \cos\left[\left(\frac{\pi}{2} - a\right) - b\right]$$

$$\sin(a + b) = \cos\left(\frac{\pi}{2} - a\right)\cos b + \sin\left(\frac{\pi}{2} - a\right)\sin b \longrightarrow \boxed{\sin(a + b) = \sin a \cos b + \cos a \sin b}$$

Similarly, to find the sine difference identity, substitute **b** for **-b** and simplify.

$$\sin(a + (-b)) = \sin a \cos(-b) + \cos a \sin(-b)$$

$$\boxed{\sin(a - b) = \sin a \cos b - \cos a \sin b}$$

To find the tangent identities, use the reciprocal identity such that $\tan(a + b) = \dfrac{\sin(a + b)}{\cos(a + b)}$ and substitute the numerator and denominator for their identities. Then, divide the numerator and denominator by the term $\cos a \cos b$ (or multiply $\sec a \sec b$) to make the expression in terms of only $\tan a$ and $\tan b$.

$$\tan(a + b) = \frac{\sin(a + b)}{\cos(a + b)} \longrightarrow \tan(a + b) = \frac{\sin a \cos b + \cos a \sin b}{\cos a \cos b - \sin a \sin b}\left(\frac{\sec a \sec b}{\sec a \sec b}\right)$$

$$\tan(a + b) = \frac{\dfrac{\sin a \cos b}{\cos a \cos b} + \dfrac{\cos a \sin b}{\cos a \cos b}}{\dfrac{\cos a \cos b}{\cos a \cos b} - \dfrac{\sin a \sin b}{\cos a \cos b}} \longrightarrow \boxed{\tan(a + b) = \frac{\tan a + \tan b}{1 - \tan a \tan b}}$$

Similarly, to find the tangent difference identity, substitute **b** for **-b** and simplify.

$$\tan(a + (-b)) = \frac{\tan a + \tan(-b)}{1 - \tan a \tan(-b)} \qquad \boxed{\tan(a - b) = \frac{\tan a - \tan b}{1 + \tan a \tan b}}$$

Sum & Difference Identities

$$\sin(a \pm b) = \sin a \cos b \pm \sin b \cos a$$

$$\cos(a \pm b) = \cos a \cos b \mp \sin a \sin b$$

$$\tan(a \pm b) = \frac{\tan a \pm \tan b}{1 \mp \tan a \tan b}$$

The $\pm$ and $\mp$ symbols represent when a plus or minus is used in an expression. If a $\pm$ and $\pm$ are in the same equation, this means that if a positive sign is chosen on the left, the **same (positive) sign** is chosen on the right. If a $\pm$ and $\mp$ are in the same equation, this means that if a positive sign is chosen on the left, the **opposite (negative) sign** is chosen on the right or vice versa.

i.e. $\cos(a + b) = \cos a \cos b - \sin a \sin b$

$\cos(a - b) = \cos a \cos b + \sin a \sin b$

After proving these identities, let's apply them in the following problem.

Example 1 — Evaluate $\sec(75°)$ using identities.

First, we must convert the expression $\sec(75°)$ in terms of cosine: $\dfrac{1}{\cos(75°)}$.
Then, since 75° is not an angle with a special trigonometric ratio, it can be broken up into two angles with special trigonometric ratios: $\dfrac{1}{\cos(30° + 45°)}$.
Use the cosine sum identity to evaluate.

$$\frac{1}{\cos(30° + 45°)} = \frac{1}{\cos 30° \cos 45° - \sin 30° \sin 45°} = \frac{1}{\frac{\sqrt{3}}{2} \cdot \frac{\sqrt{2}}{2} - \frac{1}{2} \cdot \frac{\sqrt{2}}{2}}$$

$$\frac{1}{\frac{\sqrt{6} - \sqrt{2}}{4}} = \frac{4}{\sqrt{6} - \sqrt{2}}\left(\frac{\sqrt{6} + \sqrt{2}}{\sqrt{6} + \sqrt{2}}\right) = \frac{4(\sqrt{6} + \sqrt{2})}{4} = \sqrt{6} + \sqrt{2}$$

Example 2 — Evaluate $\tan(a - b)$ if $\sin a = \dfrac{5}{6}$ and $\csc b = 3$.
$$0 < a < \frac{\pi}{2}, \, 0 < b < \frac{\pi}{2}$$

To start, let's draw two triangles for angles **a** and **b**. If the sine of **a** is 5/6, then the opposite side is 5 and the hypotenuse is 6, and using Pythagorean theorem, the adjacent side is $\sqrt{11}$.
Similarly, $\csc b = 3$ can be rewritten as $\csc b = \dfrac{3}{1}$, so the triangle with angle **b** will have a hypotenuse of 3 and opposite side of 1.

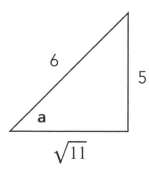

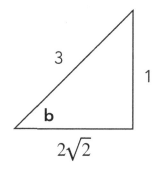

By using the tangent difference identity, we notice the formula only requires the tangent of both ratios. Using the triangles on the left, we can find the tangent of **a** & **b** and substitute it into the identity and evaluate.

$$\tan a = \frac{5}{\sqrt{11}} \qquad \tan b = \frac{1}{2\sqrt{2}}$$

$$\tan(a-b) = \frac{\tan a - \tan b}{1 + \tan a \tan b} \quad \longrightarrow \quad \tan(a-b) = \frac{\dfrac{5}{\sqrt{11}} - \dfrac{1}{2\sqrt{2}}}{1 + \dfrac{5}{\sqrt{11}} \cdot \dfrac{1}{2\sqrt{2}}}$$

$$\tan(a-b) = \frac{\dfrac{10\sqrt{2} - \sqrt{11}}{2\sqrt{22}}}{\dfrac{2\sqrt{22} + 5}{2\sqrt{22}}} \quad \longrightarrow \quad \tan(a-b) = \frac{10\sqrt{2} - \sqrt{11}}{2\sqrt{22} + 5}$$

Q **Example 3**   **Evaluate** $\cos(b-a)$ **if** $\sin a = \dfrac{5}{6}$ **and** $\cot b = -\dfrac{1}{4}$.
$$\frac{\pi}{2} < a < \frac{3\pi}{2}, \ \pi < b < 2\pi$$

This example differs from the previous one since it involves negative trigonometric ratios and different domain restrictions. Therefore, when considering each provided ratio, the quadrant of the angle must be found.

If $\sin a = \dfrac{5}{6}$ and **a** is either in Q2 or Q3, then **a** must be in Q2 since Q1 & Q2 are the only quadrants where sine is positive.

This means that the opposite side is 5 and hypotenuse is 6, and since the angle is in Q2 where cosine is **negative**, the adjacent side is $-\sqrt{6^2 - 5^2}$ or $-\sqrt{11}$.

Similarly, for angle **b**, cotangent can only be negative in Q2 or Q4. Since the domain is only restricted to Q3 & Q4, the angle must be in Q4. Therefore, the cosine is **positive** and sine is **negative**, and the adjacent side is 1, the opposite side is -4, and hypotenuse is $\sqrt{1^2 + (-4)^2}$ or $\sqrt{17}$. These triangles are illustrated below.

$$\cos(b - a) = \cos b \cos a + \sin b \sin a$$

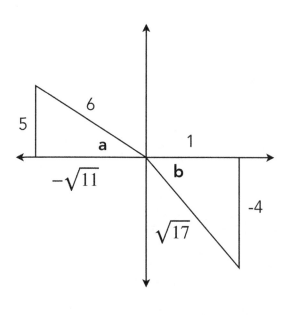

Using the information provided in the diagram, the cosine and sine of each angle can be deduced to substitute in the above identity.

$$\cos a = -\frac{\sqrt{11}}{6} \quad \cos b = \frac{1}{\sqrt{17}}$$

$$\sin a = \frac{5}{6} \quad \sin b = -\frac{4}{\sqrt{17}}$$

$$\cos(b - a) = \left(\frac{1}{\sqrt{17}}\right)\left(-\frac{\sqrt{11}}{6}\right) + \left(-\frac{4}{\sqrt{17}}\right)\left(\frac{5}{6}\right)$$

$$\cos(b - a) = \frac{-\sqrt{11} - 20}{6\sqrt{17}}$$

6.3 Practice Problems

For #1-5, evaluate the expression using the sum and difference identities.

1 $\cos\left(\dfrac{7\pi}{12}\right)$

2 $\tan(15°)$

3 $\csc\left(-\dfrac{17\pi}{12}\right)$

4 $\cot\left(5x - \dfrac{13\pi}{4}\right)$

5 $\cos(24°)\sin(51°) + \cos(51°)\sin(24°)$

For #6-9, evaluate the expression with the given ratios.

6 $\csc(a - b)$, $\sin a = 0.5$, $\cot b = 9$
$0 < a < \dfrac{\pi}{2}$, $0 < b < \dfrac{\pi}{2}$

7 $\tan(a + b)$, $\sec a = -\dfrac{4}{3}$, $\cos b = -\dfrac{2}{5}$
$\pi < a < 2\pi$, $\dfrac{\pi}{2} < b < \pi$

8 $\cos(a + k)$, $\sin a = -\dfrac{3}{10}$, $\tan k = \dfrac{7}{2}$
$\dfrac{3\pi}{2} < a < 2\pi$, $0 < b < \dfrac{\pi}{2}$

9 $\sec\left(-\dfrac{11\pi}{12} - x\right)$, $\cos x = \dfrac{5}{7}$
$\dfrac{\pi}{2} < x < \dfrac{3\pi}{2}$

For #10-12, simplify the expression.

10 $\sec x \csc y \cos(x + y)$

11 $\tan(2\pi - x)$

12 $\dfrac{\sin(\theta + \alpha) - \sin(\theta - \alpha)}{\cos(\theta - \alpha) + \cos(\theta + \alpha)}$

6.4 Double & Half Angle Identities

In this lesson 6.4, we will explore more trigonometric identities called the double angle, half angle, and power reducing formulas which can all be derived from the sum and difference identities. Let's take a look at how this works.

 ## Double Angle Proof

To begin, notice this sine sum identity:
$\sin(a + b) = \sin a \cos b + \cos a \sin b$.

Double angle identities analyze the trigonometric ratios of two times an angle, i.e. $\sin(2\theta)$. The term 2θ can be broken down simply into the sum of $\theta + \theta$. This means that $\sin(2\theta) = \sin(\theta + \theta)$ and the sine sum identity can be applied such that θ is substituted for **a** & **b**.

$$\sin(\theta + \theta) = \sin \theta \cos \theta + \cos \theta \sin \theta$$

$$\sin(2\theta) = 2 \sin \theta \cos \theta$$

That's it! Let's repeat the same process for the tangent and cosine identity by simplifying the expression $\tan(2\theta) = \tan(\theta + \theta)$ and $\cos(2\theta) = \cos(\theta + \theta)$.

$$\tan(\theta + \theta) = \frac{\tan \theta + \tan \theta}{1 - \tan \theta \tan \theta}$$

$$\cos(\theta + \theta) = \cos \theta \cos \theta - \sin \theta \sin \theta$$

$$\tan(2\theta) = \frac{2 \tan \theta}{1 - \tan^2 \theta}$$

$$\cos(2\theta) = \cos^2 \theta - \sin^2 \theta$$

However, with the double angle cosine identity, the $\cos^2 \theta$ can be substituted with $1 - \sin^2 \theta$ or the $\cos^2 \theta$ can be substituted with $1 - \cos^2 \theta$ using the Pythagorean identities. Therefore, there are 3 identities associated with $\cos(2\theta)$.

$$\cos(2\theta) = (1 - \sin^2 \theta) - \sin^2 \theta \longrightarrow \cos(2\theta) = 1 - 2 \sin^2 \theta$$

$$\cos(2\theta) = \cos^2 \theta - \sin^2 \theta$$

$$\cos(2\theta) = \cos^2 \theta - (1 - \cos^2 \theta) \longrightarrow \cos(2\theta) = 2 \cos^2 \theta - 1$$

Half Angle Proof

Half angle identities analyze the trigonometric ratios when an angle is divided by 2, i.e. $\sin\left(\dfrac{\theta}{2}\right)$. For this proof, we will utilize the 3 variations of the cosine double angle identity. Using the identity $\cos(2\alpha) = 1 - 2\sin^2\alpha$, we can define $\alpha = \dfrac{\theta}{2}$ and substitute α for $\dfrac{\theta}{2}$ to isolate $\sin\left(\dfrac{\theta}{2}\right)$ as shown below.

$$\cos(2\alpha) = 1 - 2\sin^2\alpha \;\longrightarrow\; \cos\left(2 \cdot \frac{\theta}{2}\right) = 1 - 2\sin^2\left(\frac{\theta}{2}\right) \;\longrightarrow\; \cos\theta = 1 - 2\sin^2\left(\frac{\theta}{2}\right)$$

$$\cos\theta - 1 = -2\sin^2\left(\frac{\theta}{2}\right) \longrightarrow \frac{1 - \cos\theta}{2} = \sin^2\left(\frac{\theta}{2}\right) \longrightarrow \sin\left(\frac{\theta}{2}\right) = \pm\sqrt{\frac{1 - \cos\theta}{2}}$$

This same process can be repeated with $\cos(2\alpha) = 2\cos^2\alpha - 1$ where $\alpha = \dfrac{\theta}{2}$.

$$\cos(2\alpha) = 2\cos^2\alpha - 1 \;\longrightarrow\; \cos\left(2 \cdot \frac{\theta}{2}\right) = 2\cos^2\left(\frac{\theta}{2}\right) - 1 \;\longrightarrow\; \cos\theta = 2\cos^2\left(\frac{\theta}{2}\right) - 1$$

$$\frac{1 + \cos\theta}{2} = \cos^2\left(\frac{\theta}{2}\right) \;\longrightarrow\; \cos\left(\frac{\theta}{2}\right) = \pm\sqrt{\frac{1 + \cos\theta}{2}}$$

The reciprocal identity can be used to then find $\tan\left(\dfrac{\theta}{2}\right)$.

$$\tan\left(\frac{\theta}{2}\right) = \frac{\pm\sqrt{\dfrac{1-\cos\theta}{2}}}{\pm\sqrt{\dfrac{1+\cos\theta}{2}}} \longrightarrow \tan\left(\frac{\theta}{2}\right) = \sqrt{\frac{1-\cos\theta}{2} \cdot \frac{2}{1+\cos\theta}}$$

$$\longrightarrow \tan\left(\frac{\theta}{2}\right) = \sqrt{\frac{1-\cos\theta}{1+\cos\theta}}$$

There are three variations of the $\tan\left(\dfrac{\theta}{2}\right)$ identity by multiplying $\dfrac{1-\cos\theta}{1-\cos\theta}$ or $\dfrac{1+\cos\theta}{1+\cos\theta}$.

$$\tan\left(\frac{\theta}{2}\right) = \sqrt{\frac{1-\cos\theta}{1+\cos\theta}\left(\frac{1-\cos\theta}{1-\cos\theta}\right)} \longrightarrow \tan\left(\frac{\theta}{2}\right) = \sqrt{\frac{(1-\cos\theta)^2}{\sin^2\theta}}$$

$$\longrightarrow \tan\left(\frac{\theta}{2}\right) = \frac{1-\cos\theta}{\sin\theta}$$

$$\tan\left(\frac{\theta}{2}\right) = \sqrt{\frac{1-\cos\theta}{1+\cos\theta}\left(\frac{1+\cos\theta}{1+\cos\theta}\right)} \longrightarrow \tan\left(\frac{\theta}{2}\right) = \sqrt{\frac{\sin^2\theta}{(1+\cos\theta)^2}}$$

$$\longrightarrow \tan\left(\frac{\theta}{2}\right) = \frac{\sin\theta}{1+\cos\theta}$$

Now that we have proven these identities, let's apply them in the problems on the next page.

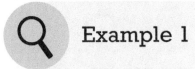 **Example 1** **Evaluate** $\cot(22.5°)$ **using identities.**

First, let's convert the cotangent expression into tangent as shown: $\dfrac{1}{\tan(22.5°)}$.

Now, to determine if a double or half angle identity should be applied for this problem, determine the value of angle θ in either $\tan\left(\dfrac{\theta}{2}\right)$ or $\tan(2\theta)$ to equal $\tan(22.5°)$.

In $\tan\left(\dfrac{\theta}{2}\right)$, θ is 45° $\tan(2\theta)$, and in $\tan(2\theta)$, θ is 11.25°. Since 45° is a special angle in which trigonometry can be performed easily, the expression $\dfrac{1}{\tan\left(\frac{45°}{2}\right)}$ will be used.

$$\cot(22.5°) = \left(\tan\left(\frac{45°}{2}\right)\right)^{-1} = \left(\frac{\sin 45°}{1+\cos 45°}\right)^{-1} = \frac{1+\cos 45°}{\sin 45°} = \frac{1+\frac{1}{\sqrt{2}}}{\frac{1}{\sqrt{2}}}\left(\frac{\sqrt{2}}{\sqrt{2}}\right)$$

$$1+\sqrt{2}$$

 Example 2 **Evaluate** $\cos(2a)$ **if** $\tan a = -0.8$ **and** $0 < a < \pi$.

Let's start this problem by finding the quadrant for angle **a**. Since the tangent is negative, **a** can be in either Q2 or Q4, but the domain of **a** is restricted to Q1 and Q2, so angle **a** must be in Q2. If $\tan a = -0.8$, which can be rewritten as $-\dfrac{4}{5}$, then the opposite side is 4 and adjacent side is -5 (since cosine is negative in Q2). Using Pythagorean Theorem, the hypotenuse is $\sqrt{41}$.

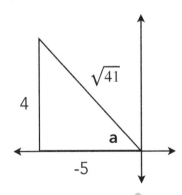

The cosine double angle identity has 3 variations. For this example, we will use $2\cos^2 a - 1$, but any other variation should produce the same answer. The cosine of **a** is $\dfrac{-5}{\sqrt{41}}$, so this can be substituted into the identity and simplified.

$$\cos(2a) = 2\cos^2 a - 1 = 2\left(\frac{-5}{\sqrt{41}}\right)^2 - 1 = \frac{50}{41} - 1 = \frac{9}{41}$$

🔍 Example 3

Evaluate $\cos\left(b - \dfrac{a}{2}\right)$ **if** $\cos a = -\dfrac{6}{7}$ **and** $\cos b = \dfrac{2}{5}$.

$$\pi < a < 2\pi, \ \pi < b < 2\pi$$

This complex problem contains multiple identities from lessons 6.3 and 6.4.

To begin with, let's expand the expression using the cosine difference formula as shown:

$$\cos b \cos(a/2) + \sin b \sin(a/2)$$

Then, we can apply the half angle identities for cosine and sine to create:

$$\cos b\left(\pm\sqrt{\frac{1 + \cos a}{2}}\right) + \sin b\left(\pm\sqrt{\frac{1 - \cos a}{2}}\right)$$

The problem already provides the cosine values for **a** and **b**, so all we need to find is $\sin b$. Angle **b** has a positive cosine, so it can be in Q1 or Q4, but since the domain is restricted to Q3 & Q4, angle **b** must be in Q4.

When we draw a triangle for angle **b**, the adjacent side is 2, the hypotenuse is 5, and the opposite side is calculated as $-\sqrt{21}$ since sine is negative in Q4.

$$\sin b = \frac{-\sqrt{21}}{5}$$

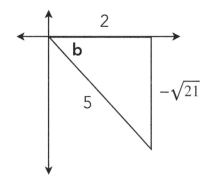

After finding $\sin b$, we can now substitute all values into the above expression.

$$\left(\frac{2}{5}\right)\left(\pm\sqrt{\frac{1 - \frac{6}{7}}{2}}\right) + \left(\frac{-\sqrt{21}}{5}\right)\left(\pm\sqrt{\frac{1 + \frac{6}{7}}{2}}\right)$$

$$= \left(\frac{2}{5}\right)\left(\pm\sqrt{\frac{1}{14}}\right) + \left(\frac{-\sqrt{21}}{5}\right)\left(\pm\sqrt{\frac{13}{14}}\right)$$

Before continuing to simplify this expression, we must determine whether to use the positive or negative square root, since it is currently ±. To find this, let's first analyze the domain of angle **a** in $\cos(a/2)$ and $\sin(a/2)$.

Since angle **a** has a negative cosine value, it can be in either Q2 or Q3. However, the problem restricts the domain of **a** in Q3 and Q4, so angle **a** must be in Q3. Therefore, the actual domain of angle **a** can be written as below:

$$\pi < a < \frac{3\pi}{2}$$

To determine the domain of $\frac{a}{2}$, we can divide each term by 2 in the inequality to receive the following domain:

$$\frac{\pi}{2} < \frac{a}{2} < \frac{3\pi}{4}$$

This domain shows that the angle $\frac{a}{2}$ is restricted in Q2 since the interval $\left(\frac{\pi}{2}, \frac{3\pi}{4}\right)$ is within the Q2 interval $\left(\frac{\pi}{2}, \pi\right)$. Therefore, the angle will have a **positive** sine and **negative** cosine.

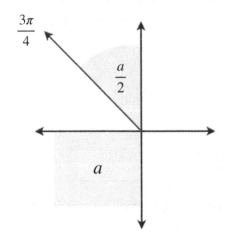

$$\left(\frac{2}{5}\right)\left(\pm\sqrt{\frac{1}{14}}\right) + \left(\frac{-\sqrt{21}}{5}\right)\left(\pm\sqrt{\frac{13}{14}}\right)$$

$$\uparrow \qquad\qquad\qquad\qquad \uparrow$$

$$\cos(a/2) \qquad\qquad\qquad \sin(a/2)$$

$$= \left(\frac{2}{5}\right)\left(-\sqrt{\frac{1}{14}}\right) + \left(\frac{-\sqrt{21}}{5}\right)\left(\sqrt{\frac{13}{14}}\right)$$

$$= \frac{-2 - \sqrt{273}}{5\sqrt{14}}$$

6.4 Practice Problems

For #1-5, evaluate the expression using the double and half angle identities.

1 $\cos\left(\dfrac{\pi}{12}\right)$

2 $\cot(22.5°)$

3 $\sin(67.5°)$

4 $\csc\left(\dfrac{13\pi}{16}\right)$

5 $\dfrac{4\tan\left(\frac{5\pi}{8}\right)}{\tan^2\left(\frac{5\pi}{8}\right) - 1}$

For #6-9, evaluate the expression with the given ratios.

6 $\sec\left(\dfrac{x}{2}\right)$, $\cot x = 1.2$, $\pi < x < \dfrac{3\pi}{2}$

7 $\tan(2a - b)$, $\cos a = -\dfrac{6}{7}$, $\csc b = \dfrac{9}{8}$

$\dfrac{\pi}{2} < a < \pi$, $0 < b < \dfrac{\pi}{2}$

8 $\sin(4\theta)$, $\sec\theta = 10$, $\dfrac{3\pi}{2} < \theta < 2\pi$

9 $\cot(10\pi + 2x)$, $\csc x = \dfrac{8}{5}$

$\dfrac{\pi}{2} < x < \pi$

For #10-12, verify the identity.

10 $[4\sin(2\alpha)\cos(2\alpha)][1 - 2\sin^2(2\alpha)]$

11 $\left[\cos\left(\dfrac{w}{2}\right) + \sin\left(\dfrac{w}{2}\right)\right]^2$

12 $4\sin^2\left(\dfrac{\theta}{2}\right)\cos^2\left(\dfrac{\theta}{2}\right)$

6.5 Power Reducing Identities

In this final lesson, we will learn how to manipulate the double angle identities to create a new set of identities called power reducing identities. Power reducing identities are used to rewrite trigonometric ratios (ex. $\cos^3(x)$) in terms of smaller powers (ex. $\cos^2 x$ and $\cos x$).

 ## Power Reducing Proof

This proof is fairly straightforward as it simply re-arranges terms in each of the different versions of the cosine double angle identity.

$$\cos(2\theta) = 1 - 2\sin^2\theta$$

$$2\sin^2\theta = 1 - \cos(2\theta)$$

$$\sin^2\theta = \frac{1 - \cos(2\theta)}{2}$$

For example, for finding the power reducing formula for $\sin^2\theta$, we can rearrange the terms in the identity $\cos(2\theta) = 1 - 2\sin^2\theta$.

Similarly, we can repeat this process for $\cos^2\theta$ by isolating $\cos^2\theta$ in $\cos(2\theta) = 2\cos^2\theta + 1$. For $\tan^2\theta$, we can use the reciprocal identity to divide $\sin^2\theta$ by $\cos^2\theta$.

$$\cos(2\theta) = 2\cos^2\theta - 1 \longrightarrow 2\cos^2\theta = 1 + \cos(2\theta) \longrightarrow \cos^2\theta = \frac{1 + \cos(2\theta)}{2}$$

$$\tan^2\theta = \frac{\sin^2\theta}{\cos^2\theta} \longrightarrow \tan^2\theta = \frac{\frac{1 - \cos(2\theta)}{2}}{\frac{1 + \cos(2\theta)}{2}} \longrightarrow \tan^2\theta = \frac{1 - \cos(2\theta)}{1 + \cos(2\theta)}$$

As mentioned above, the goal of these identities is to rewrite trigonometric functions in smaller powers, hence called power reducing identities. For example, the $\sin^2\theta$ identity reduces the power of the ratio from 2 to 1 by rewriting it in terms of $\cos(2\theta)$.
Let's apply this in the following examples on the next page.

Q ## Example 1   **Simplify $3\tan^4\theta$ in terms of reduced powers.**

To begin, lets identify which power reducing identity we will be using. Since this is in terms of tangent, we will use $\tan^2\theta = \dfrac{1-\cos(2\theta)}{1+\cos(2\theta)}$. To utilize this identity, we need to rewrite $3\tan^4\theta$ as $3(\tan^2\theta)^2$. Then, we can substitute $\tan^2\theta$ for the above identity and simplify.

$$3(\tan^2\theta)^2 \longrightarrow 3\left(\frac{1-\cos(2\theta)}{1+\cos(2\theta)}\right)^2 \longrightarrow 3\left(\frac{[1-\cos(2\theta)]\cdot[1-\cos(2\theta)]}{[1+\cos(2\theta)]\cdot[1+\cos(2\theta)]}\right)$$

Substitute $\tan^2\theta$ Expand the squared fraction

$$\longrightarrow 3\left(\frac{1-2\cos(2\theta)+\cos^2(2\theta)}{1+2\cos(2\theta)+\cos^2(2\theta)}\right)$$

Binomial expansion

This expression can be further simplified since the $\cos(2\theta)$ is still squared. Therefore, we can utilize the power reducing cosine identity: $\cos^2\theta = \dfrac{1+\cos(2\theta)}{2}$. However, for this expression, the θ in the identity must be substituted for 2θ, resulting in:
$\cos^2(2\theta) = \dfrac{1+\cos(2\cdot(2\theta))}{2} = \cos^2(2\theta) = \dfrac{1+\cos(4\theta)}{2}$. Let's substitute this identity into the expression above and simplify.

$$3\left(\frac{1-2\cos(2\theta)+\cos^2(2\theta)}{1+2\cos(2\theta)+\cos^2(2\theta)}\right) \longrightarrow 3\left(\frac{1-2\cos(2\theta)+\frac{1+\cos(4\theta)}{2}}{1+2\cos(2\theta)+\frac{1+\cos(4\theta)}{2}}\right)\left(\frac{2}{2}\right)$$

Substitute $\cos^2(2\theta)$

$$\longrightarrow 3\left(\frac{2-4\cos(2\theta)+1+\cos(4\theta)}{2+4\cos(2\theta)+1+\cos(4\theta)}\right) \longrightarrow \frac{9-12\cos(2\theta)+3\cos(4\theta)}{3+4\cos(2\theta)+\cos(4\theta)}$$

Simplify complex fraction   Multiply by 3 and simplify.

145

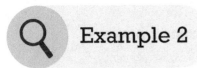 **Example 2** **Simplify $\sec^3 \alpha \sin \alpha$ in terms of reduced powers.**

First, let's identify the power reducing identity we should use. Since $\sec^3 \alpha$ can be written as a reciprocal $\dfrac{1}{\cos^3 \alpha}$, the cosine identity that can be used is: $\cos^2 \theta = \dfrac{1 + \cos(2\theta)}{2}$.

To utilize this identity, we need to rewrite $\cos^3 \alpha$ as $\cos \alpha \cdot \cos^2 \alpha$ and then substitute $\cos^2 \theta$ for the above identity and simplify.

$$\sec^3 \alpha \sin \alpha \longrightarrow \frac{1}{\cos \alpha \cdot \cos^2 \alpha} \cdot \sin \alpha \longrightarrow \frac{\sin \alpha}{\cos \alpha \cdot \frac{1 + \cos(2\alpha)}{2}}$$

Rewritten to substitute $\cos^2 \alpha$ Substitute $\cos^2 \alpha$

$$\frac{2 \sin \alpha}{\cos \alpha \cdot [1 + \cos(2\alpha)]} \longrightarrow \frac{2 \tan \alpha}{1 + \cos(2\alpha)}$$

Simplify complex fraction   Quotient Identity

NOTE

You may notice in practice problems that trigonometric functions raised to an odd power (such as $\tan^3 x$ or $\sin^5 x$), it is difficult to reduce the powers to 1 using the above formulas.

By manipulating the $\sin(3x)$, $\cos(3x)$, and $\tan(3x)$ identities (similar to the proof for the other power reducing formulas), the following formulas are created and may be used in some circumstances:

$$\sin^3 x = \frac{3}{4} \sin x - \frac{1}{4} \sin 3x \qquad\qquad \cos^3 x = \frac{3}{4} \cos x + \frac{1}{4} \cos 3x$$

$$\tan^3 x = \frac{3 \sin x - \sin(3x)}{3 \cos x + \cos(3x)}$$

6.5 Practice Problems

For #1-5, expand or simplify the expression in terms of reduced powers.

1 $2\sec^4 x$

2 $4\sin^2 x \cot^4 x$

3 $3\csc^2\left(\dfrac{7\pi}{8}\right)$

4 $\cos^2\left(\dfrac{5\pi}{16}\right) - \sin^2\left(\dfrac{11\pi}{16}\right)$

5 $\tan^4(2x)$

For #6-7, evaluate the expression with the given ratios.

6 $\cos^2\alpha,\ \sin(2\alpha) = 0.9,\ 0 < \alpha < \dfrac{\pi}{2}$

7 $\sin^2\left(\dfrac{\alpha}{2}\right),\ \tan\alpha = -\dfrac{5}{4},\ \dfrac{\pi}{2} < \alpha < \pi$

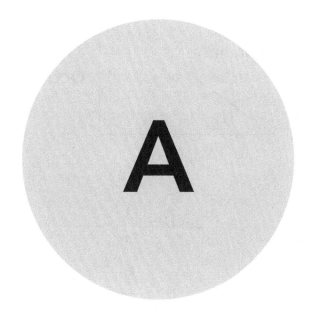

Appendix

A.1 Basic Trigonometry Reference

Trigonometric Ratios

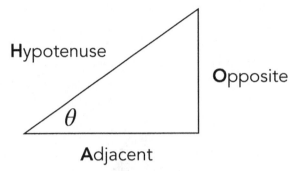

$$\sin \theta = \frac{O}{H} \qquad \cos \theta = \frac{A}{H} \qquad \tan \theta = \frac{O}{A}$$

$$\csc \theta = \frac{H}{O} \qquad \sec \theta = \frac{H}{A} \qquad \cot \theta = \frac{A}{O}$$

Unit Circle

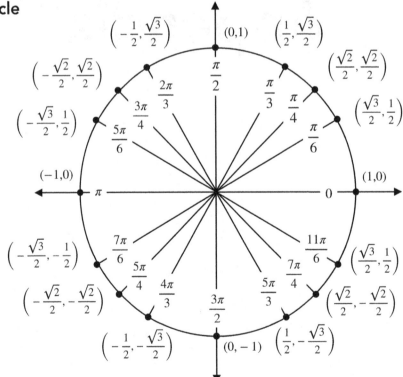

A.2 Trigonometric Graphs

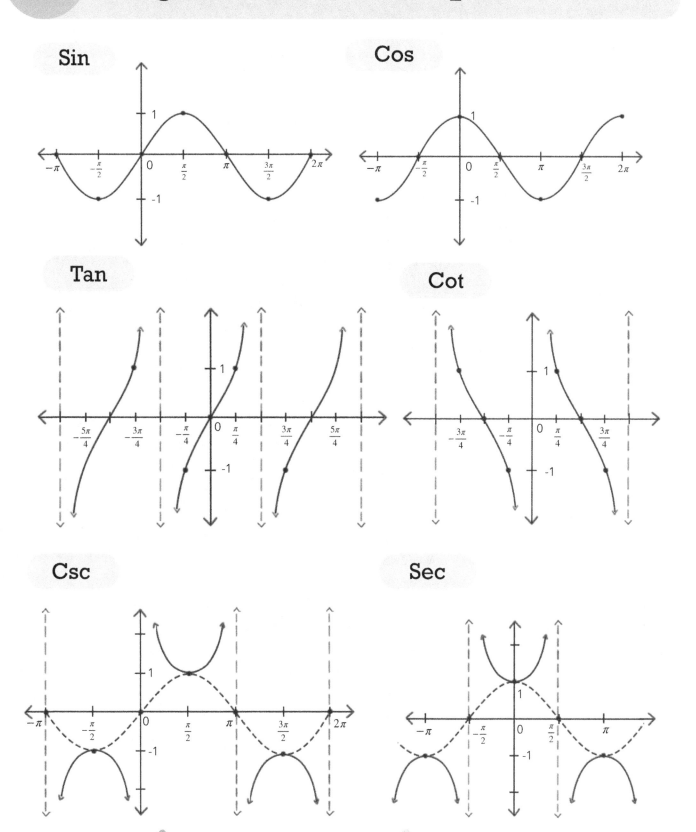

Sin

Cos

Tan

Cot

Csc

Sec

A.2 Trigonometric Graphs

Arcsin

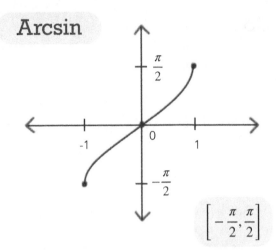

$$\left[-\frac{\pi}{2}, \frac{\pi}{2}\right]$$

Arccos

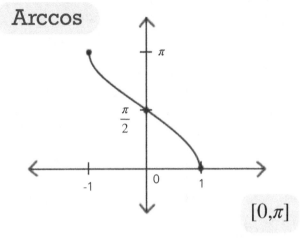

$$[0, \pi]$$

Arctan

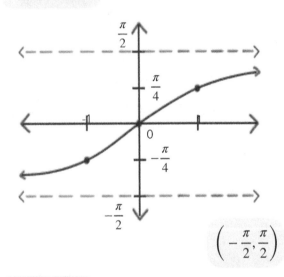

$$\left(-\frac{\pi}{2}, \frac{\pi}{2}\right)$$

Arccsc

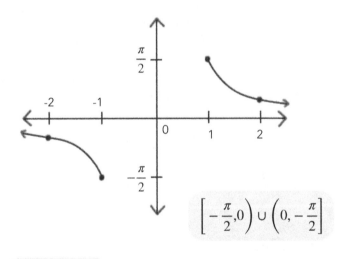

$$\left[-\frac{\pi}{2}, 0\right) \cup \left(0, -\frac{\pi}{2}\right]$$

Arcsec

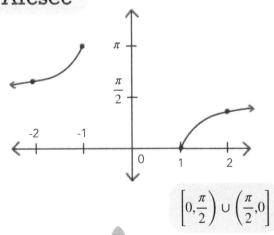

$$\left[0, \frac{\pi}{2}\right) \cup \left(\frac{\pi}{2}, 0\right]$$

Arccot

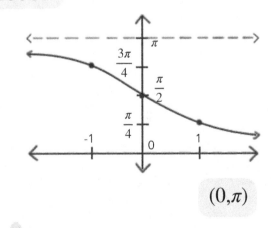

$$(0, \pi)$$

A.3 Trigonometric Identities

Quotient Identities

$$\tan\theta = \frac{\sin\theta}{\cos\theta} \qquad \cot\theta = \frac{\cos\theta}{\sin\theta}$$

Reciprocal Identities

$$\csc\theta = \frac{1}{\sin\theta} \quad \sec\theta = \frac{1}{\cos\theta} \quad \cot\theta = \frac{1}{\tan\theta}$$

Even & Odd Identities

$$\sin(-\theta) = -\sin\theta \qquad \csc(-\theta) = -\csc\theta$$

$$\cos(-\theta) = \cos\theta \qquad \sec(-\theta) = \sec\theta$$

$$\tan(-\theta) = -\tan\theta \qquad \cot(-\theta) = -\cot\theta$$

Cofunction Identities

$$\sin\left(\frac{\pi}{2} - \theta\right) = \cos\theta \quad \cos\left(\frac{\pi}{2} - \theta\right) = \sin\theta$$

$$\tan\left(\frac{\pi}{2} - \theta\right) = \cot\theta \quad \cot\left(\frac{\pi}{2} - \theta\right) = \tan\theta$$

$$\csc\left(\frac{\pi}{2} - \theta\right) = \sec\theta \quad \sec\left(\frac{\pi}{2} - \theta\right) = \csc\theta$$

Pythagorean Identities

$$\sin^2\theta + \cos^2\theta = 1 \qquad 1 + \cot^2\theta = \csc^2\theta$$

$$\tan^2\theta + 1 = \sec^2\theta$$

Sum & Difference Identities

$$\sin(a \pm b) = \sin a \cos b \pm \sin b \cos a$$

$$\cos(a \pm b) = \cos a \cos b \mp \sin a \sin b$$

$$\tan(a \pm b) = \frac{\tan a \pm \tan b}{1 \mp \tan a \tan b}$$

Double Angle Identities

$$\sin(2\theta) = 2\sin\theta\cos\theta$$

$$\cos(2\theta) = \cos^2\theta - \sin^2\theta$$

$$\cos(2\theta) = 1 - 2\sin^2\theta$$

$$\cos(2\theta) = 2\cos^2\theta - 1$$

$$\tan(2\theta) = \frac{2\tan\theta}{1 - \tan^2\theta}$$

Power Reducing Identities

$$\sin^2\theta = \frac{1 - \cos(2\theta)}{2}$$

$$\cos^2\theta = \frac{1 + \cos(2\theta)}{2}$$

$$\tan^2\theta = \frac{1 - \cos(2\theta)}{1 + \cos(2\theta)}$$

A.3 Trigonometric Identities

Half Angle Identities

$$\sin\left(\frac{\theta}{2}\right) = \pm\sqrt{\frac{1 - \cos\theta}{2}}$$

$$\cos\left(\frac{\theta}{2}\right) = \pm\sqrt{\frac{1 + \cos\theta}{2}}$$

$$\tan\left(\frac{\theta}{2}\right) = \pm\sqrt{\frac{1 - \cos\theta}{1 + \cos\theta}}$$

$$\tan\left(\frac{\theta}{2}\right) = \frac{\sin\theta}{1 + \cos\theta}$$

$$\tan\left(\frac{\theta}{2}\right) = \frac{1 - \cos\theta}{\sin\theta}$$

Sum to Product Identities

$$\sin a \pm \sin b = 2\sin\left(\frac{a \pm b}{2}\right)\cos\left(\frac{a \mp b}{2}\right)$$

$$\cos a + \cos b = 2\cos\left(\frac{a + b}{2}\right)\cos\left(\frac{a - b}{2}\right)$$

$$\cos a - \cos b = -2\sin\left(\frac{a + b}{2}\right)\sin\left(\frac{a - b}{2}\right)$$

Product to Sum Identities

$$\sin a \sin b = \frac{1}{2}[\cos(a - b) - \cos(a + b)]$$

$$\sin a \cos b = \frac{1}{2}[\sin(a + b) + \sin(a - b)]$$

$$\cos a \cos b = \frac{1}{2}[\cos(a - b) + \cos(a + b)]$$

$$\cos a \sin b = \frac{1}{2}[\sin(a + b) - \sin(a - b)]$$

Answer Key

Unit 1: Properties of Triangles

1.1 Similar Triangles &
1.2 Triangle Notation

1. No
2. No
3. Yes, SAS Theorem
4. Yes, SSS Theorem
5. Yes, AA Theorem
6. No
7. 16.2
8. 64
9. 42
10. $\dfrac{65}{27}$

1.3 Triangle Theorems

1. Yes, acute
2. No
3. Yes, right
4. No
5. Yes, obtuse
6. Yes, obtuse
7. $\overline{YZ} < \overline{XY} < \overline{XZ}$

   $X < Z < Y$
8. $\overline{XY} < \overline{YZ} < \overline{XZ}$

   $Z < X < Y$
9. $\overline{XY} < \overline{XZ} < \overline{YZ}$

   $Z < Y < X$
10. $\overline{XZ} < \overline{YZ} < \overline{XY}$

    $Y < X < Z$

Unit 2: Right Triangle Trigonometry

2.1 Special Triangles

1. a=10, b=10, $c = 10\sqrt{2}$, d=7, e=14, $f = 7\sqrt{3}$

2. $a = \dfrac{15\sqrt{2}}{2}$, $b = \dfrac{15\sqrt{2}}{2}$, c=15, d=4, e=8, $f = 4\sqrt{3}$

3. a=14, b=14, $c = 14\sqrt{2}$, $d = 4\sqrt{3}$, $e = 8\sqrt{3}$, f=12

4. $a = 5\sqrt{2}$, $b = 5\sqrt{2}$, c=10, d=6, e=12, $f = 6\sqrt{3}$

5. $a = 2\sqrt{3}$, $b = 2\sqrt{3}$, $c = 2\sqrt{6}$, $d = 2\sqrt{3}$, $e = 4\sqrt{3}$, f=6

6. $a = 8\sqrt{2}$, $b = 8\sqrt{2}$, c=16, $d = 4\sqrt{2}$, $e = 8\sqrt{2}$, $f = 4\sqrt{6}$

7. $a = 5\sqrt{6}$, $b = 5\sqrt{6}$, $c = 10\sqrt{3}$, d=10, e=20, $f = 10\sqrt{3}$

8. a=9, b=9, $c = 9\sqrt{2}$, $d = 9\sqrt{2}$, $e = 18\sqrt{2}$, $f = 9\sqrt{6}$

2.2 Trigonometric Ratios

1. $\tan A = \dfrac{4}{3}$

2. $\cos A = \dfrac{\sqrt{95}}{19}$

3. $2 \sin A = \dfrac{4}{3}$

4. $\cos A = \dfrac{11}{221}$

5. $\tan A = \dfrac{\sqrt{105}}{8}$

6. $5 \sin A = \dfrac{15\sqrt{34}}{34}$

7. $\sin A = \dfrac{4}{5}, \cos A = \dfrac{3}{5}$, $\tan A = \dfrac{4}{3}, \sin B = \dfrac{3}{5}$, $\cos B = \dfrac{4}{5}, \tan A = \dfrac{3}{4}$

8. $\sin A = \dfrac{31\sqrt{2}}{50}, \cos A = \dfrac{17\sqrt{2}}{50}$, $\tan A = \dfrac{31}{17}, \sin B = \dfrac{17\sqrt{2}}{50}$, $\cos B = \dfrac{31\sqrt{2}}{50}, \tan B = \dfrac{17}{31}$

Unit 2: Right Triangle Trigonometry

2.3 Solving for Sides

1. a=4.13
2. a=18.87
3. a=48.46
4. a=7.64
5. A=34°, b=19.57
6. A=67°, b=35.34
7. a=20.63, b=18.04
8. a=3.53, b=16.63

2.4 Inverse Trigonometry

1. A=73.3°
2. A=50.28°
3. A=41.41°
4. A=24.04°
5. A=23.58°, B=66.42°
6. A=37.57°, B=52.43°
7. A=61.93°, b=5.33
8. A=29.54°, b=16.91

2.5 Reciprocal Ratios

1. $\sin x = \dfrac{4}{9}$
2. Not possible
3. $\cot x = \dfrac{7\sqrt{12}}{12}$
4. $\cos x = \dfrac{35\sqrt{1241}}{1241}$
5. $\sin x = \dfrac{\sqrt{451}}{26}$
6. $\cos x = \dfrac{\sqrt{19}}{12}$
7. $\sec x = \dfrac{\sqrt{a^2+9}}{3}$
8. $\sin x = \dfrac{\sqrt{64-b}}{8}$
9. $\tan x = \dfrac{20\sqrt{169c^2-400}}{169c^2-400}$

2.6 Reciprocal Ratios

1. $\sin 30° = \dfrac{1}{2}$
2. $\cos 60° = \dfrac{1}{2}$
3. $\tan 45° = 1$
4. $\cot 60° = \dfrac{\sqrt{3}}{3}$
5. $\csc 45° = \sqrt{2}$
6. $\sec 30° = \dfrac{2\sqrt{3}}{3}$
7. $\cos 45° = \dfrac{\sqrt{2}}{2}$
8. $\cot 30° = \sqrt{3}$
9. $\csc 60° = \dfrac{2\sqrt{3}}{3}$

2.7 Elevation & Depression

1. 53.13°
2. 90 ft
3. 26.71 mi
4. Thomas is faster by 8.97 m/s.
5. 5.22 ft
6. 26.54 ft

Unit 3: Unit Circle Trigonometry

3.1 Radians

1. $\dfrac{7\pi}{15}$

2. 80°

3. $\dfrac{51\pi}{20}$

4. 382.5°

5. 330°

6. $\dfrac{5\pi}{6}$

7. $\dfrac{5\pi}{3}$

8. 120°

9. 225°

3.2 Angles on Coordinate Plane

1. -123° & 597°

2. 124° & -596°

3. $\dfrac{3\pi}{2}$ & $-\dfrac{\pi}{2}$

4. $\dfrac{\pi}{8}$ & $-\dfrac{15\pi}{8}$

5. $\dfrac{4\pi}{3}$ & $-\dfrac{2\pi}{3}$

6.

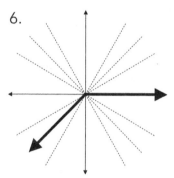

7.

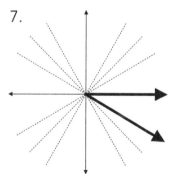

8.

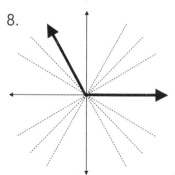

3.3 Unit Circle

1. $\cos\theta = -0.5$

2. $\csc\theta = 1.64$

3. $\cot\theta = -9.9$

4. Not possible

5. $\cot\theta = 0.51$

6. $\sec\theta = -1.10$

7. $\sin\theta = 0$

   $\cos\theta = 1$

   $\tan\theta = 0$

   $\csc\theta = $ undef.

   $\sec\theta = 1$

   $\cot\theta = $ undef.

8. $\sin\theta = -1$

   $\cos\theta = 0$

   $\tan\theta = $ undef.

   $\csc\theta = -1$

   $\sec\theta = $ undef.

   $\cot\theta = 0$

9. $\sin\theta = 1$

   $\cos\theta = 0$

   $\tan\theta = $ undef.

   $\csc\theta = 1$

   $\sec\theta = $ undef.

   $\cot\theta = 0$

Unit 3: Unit Circle Trigonometry

3.4 Special Ratios on Unit Circle

1. $\sin 30° = \dfrac{1}{2}$

2. $\cos 60° = \dfrac{1}{2}$

3. $\tan 45° = 1$

4. $\cot 60° = \dfrac{\sqrt{3}}{3}$

5. $\csc 45° = \sqrt{2}$

6. $\sec 30° = \dfrac{2\sqrt{3}}{3}$

7. $\cos 45° = \dfrac{\sqrt{2}}{2}$

8. $\cot 30° = \sqrt{3}$

9. $\csc 60° = \dfrac{2\sqrt{3}}{3}$

3.5 Ratios of Any Angle

1. $\sin 300° = -\dfrac{\sqrt{3}}{2}$

2. $\cos\left(-\dfrac{3\pi}{4}\right) = -\dfrac{\sqrt{2}}{2}$

3. $\tan\dfrac{4\pi}{3} = \sqrt{3}$

4. $\cot\dfrac{5\pi}{6} = -\sqrt{3}$

5. $\csc\left(-\dfrac{\pi}{3}\right) = -\dfrac{2\sqrt{3}}{3}$

6. $\sec\left(-\dfrac{3\pi}{2}\right) = $ undef.

7. $\cos\left(\dfrac{11\pi}{4}\right) = -\dfrac{\sqrt{2}}{2}$

8. $\sin(-720°) = 0$

9. $\csc\left(\dfrac{13\pi}{6}\right) = 2$

10. $\cos\theta = -\dfrac{7\sqrt{130}}{130}$

11. $\tan\theta = -\dfrac{5}{8}$

12. $\csc\theta = -\dfrac{\sqrt{37}}{6}$

3.6 Trigonometric Equations

1. $x = \dfrac{2\pi}{3}, \dfrac{4\pi}{3}$

2. $x = \dfrac{\pi}{6}, \dfrac{5\pi}{6}, \dfrac{7\pi}{6}, \dfrac{11\pi}{6}$

3. $x = 0, \dfrac{\pi}{4}, \pi, \dfrac{5\pi}{4}$

4. $x = \dfrac{\pi}{6}, \dfrac{7\pi}{6}$

5. $x = \pm\, 1.107$ rad

6. $x = 0, \dfrac{\pi}{12}, \dfrac{\pi}{3}, \dfrac{\pi}{4}, \dfrac{5\pi}{12}$

Unit 4: Trigonometric Graphs

For Chapter 4, please use a graphing calculator to check your sketch/graph.

4.1 Sine & Cosine Graphs

1. Period: 8π

   Amplitude: 1

   Vert. Reflect: yes

   Midline: $y = 1$

   Horiz. Shift: none

2. Period: $\dfrac{\pi}{2}$

   Amplitude: 3

   Vert. Reflect: no

   Midline: $y = -2$

   Horiz. Shift: $\dfrac{\pi}{2}$ left

3. Period: $\dfrac{6\pi}{5}$

   Amplitude: 2

   Vert. Reflect: yes

   Midline: $y = 0$

   Horiz. Shift: $\dfrac{2\pi}{5}$ left

4. Period: $\dfrac{\pi}{3}$

   Amplitude: $\dfrac{3}{2}$

   Vert. Reflect: no

   Midline: $y = \dfrac{1}{2}$

   Horiz. Shift: $\dfrac{5\pi}{6}$ right

5. Period: 2

   Amplitude: $\dfrac{\pi}{2}$

   Vert. Reflect: yes

   Midline: $y = -2\pi$

   Horiz. Shift: $\dfrac{5}{2}$ right

6. Period: $\dfrac{\pi}{3}$

   Amplitude: 8

   Vert. Reflect: no

   Midline: $y = 0$

   Horiz. Shift: $\dfrac{\pi}{3}$ right

7. Period: $\dfrac{5\pi}{4}$

   Amplitude: 4

   Vert. Reflect: yes

   Midline: $y = 6$

   Horiz. Shift: $\dfrac{5\pi}{2}$ left

8. Period: $\dfrac{\pi}{8}$

   Amplitude: 3

   Vert. Reflect: no

   Midline: $y = -4$

   Horiz. Shift: $\dfrac{5\pi}{8}$ right

Unit 4: Trigonometric Graphs

4.2 Tangent & Cotangent Graphs

1. Period: $\dfrac{2\pi}{3}$

   Vert. Stretch: 3

   Vert. Reflect: yes

   Vert. Shift: 2 up

   Horiz. Shift: none

   Asymp: $x = \dfrac{\pi}{3} + \dfrac{2\pi}{3}n$

2. Period: $\dfrac{\pi}{6}$

   Vert. Stretch: 5

   Vert. Reflect: no

   Vert. Shift: 1 down

   Horiz. Shift: $\dfrac{\pi}{3}$ left

   Asymp: $x = \dfrac{\pi}{6}n$

3. Period: $\dfrac{2\pi}{7}$

   Vert. Stretch: 4

   Vert. Reflect: yes

   Vert. Shift: none

   Horiz. Shift: $\dfrac{\pi}{7}$ left

   Asymp: $x = \dfrac{\pi}{7} + \dfrac{2\pi}{7}n$

4. Period: $\dfrac{\pi}{4}$

   Vert. Stretch: $\dfrac{5}{4}$

   Vert. Reflect: no

   Vert. Shift: $\dfrac{5}{2}$ up

   Horiz. Shift: $\dfrac{\pi}{4}$ right

   Asymp: $x = \dfrac{\pi}{8} + \dfrac{\pi}{4}n$

5. Period: 8

   Vert. Stretch: $\dfrac{5\pi}{2}$

   Vert. Reflect: yes

   Vert. Shift: π down

   Horiz. Shift: 2 right

   Asymp: $x = 6 + 8n$

6. Period: $\dfrac{7\pi}{6}$

   Vert. Stretch: 5

   Vert. Reflect: no

   Vert. Shift: none

   Horiz. Shift: $\dfrac{\pi}{3}$ right

   Asymp: $x = \dfrac{\pi}{3} + \dfrac{7\pi}{6}n$

7. Period: $\dfrac{4\pi}{3}$

   Vert. Stretch: 3

   Vert. Reflect: yes

   Vert. Shift: 1 up

   Horiz. Shift: 6π left

   Asymp: $x = \dfrac{2\pi}{3} + \dfrac{4\pi}{3}n$

8. Period: $\dfrac{\pi}{4}$

   Vert. Stretch: 9

   Vert. Reflect: no

   Vert. Shift: 4 down

   Horiz. Shift: $\dfrac{5\pi}{8}$ right

   Asymp: $x = \dfrac{\pi}{4}n$

Unit 4: Trigonometric Graphs

4.3 Cosecant & Secant Graphs

1. Period: 3π
    Vert. Stretch: 9
    Vert. Reflect: yes
    Vert. Shift: 3 up
    Horiz. Shift: none
    Asymp: $x = \dfrac{3\pi}{2}n$

2. Period: π
    Vert. Stretch: 2
    Vert. Reflect: no
    Vert. Shift: 4 down
    Horiz. Shift: $\dfrac{3\pi}{2}$ left
    Asymp: $x = \dfrac{\pi}{2} + \dfrac{\pi}{4}n$

3. Period: 8π
    Vert. Stretch: 2
    Vert. Reflect: yes
    Vert. Shift: none
    Horiz. Shift: 3π left
    Asymp: $x = 3\pi + 4\pi n$

4. Period: $\dfrac{\pi}{2}$
    Vert. Stretch: $\dfrac{2}{3}$
    Vert. Reflect: no
    Vert. Shift: $\dfrac{1}{3}$ up
    Horiz. Shift: $\dfrac{\pi}{4}$ right
    Asymp: $x = \dfrac{\pi}{4}n$

5. Period: 1
    Vert. Stretch: $\dfrac{\pi}{2}$
    Vert. Reflect: yes
    Vert. Shift: π down
    Horiz. Shift: $\dfrac{3}{2}$ right
    Asymp: $x = \dfrac{1}{2}n$

6. Period: $\dfrac{\pi}{2}$
    Vert. Stretch: 2
    Vert. Reflect: no
    Vert. Shift: none
    Horiz. Shift: $\dfrac{5\pi}{4}$ right
    Asymp: $x = \dfrac{\pi}{8} + \dfrac{\pi}{4}n$

7. Period: $\dfrac{8\pi}{7}$
    Vert. Stretch: 3
    Vert. Reflect: yes
    Vert. Shift: 5 up
    Horiz. Shift: $\dfrac{12\pi}{7}$ left
    Asymp: $x = \dfrac{2\pi}{7} + \dfrac{4\pi}{7}n$

8. Period: $\dfrac{\pi}{3}$
    Vert. Stretch: 3
    Vert. Reflect: no
    Vert. Shift: 1 down
    Horiz. Shift: $\dfrac{\pi}{12}$ right
    Asymp: $x = \dfrac{\pi}{12} + \dfrac{\pi}{6}n$

4.4 Equations from Graphs

1. $y = -2\cos(3x) - 1$

    $y = -2\sin\left(3x - \dfrac{3\pi}{2}\right) - 1$

2. $y = -\tan\left(\dfrac{1}{2}x - \dfrac{3\pi}{8}\right) + 1$

    $y = \cot\left(\dfrac{1}{2}x - \dfrac{7\pi}{8}\right) + 1$

3. $y = -\dfrac{1}{2}\sec\left(\dfrac{4}{3}x + \dfrac{\pi}{6}\right) - \dfrac{1}{2}$

    $y = \dfrac{1}{2}\csc\left(\dfrac{4}{3}x - \dfrac{\pi}{3}\right) - \dfrac{1}{2}$

4. $y = 2\tan\left(\dfrac{\pi}{3}x - \dfrac{\pi}{6}\right)$

    $y = -2\cot\left(\dfrac{\pi}{3}x - \dfrac{2\pi}{3}\right)$

Unit 4: Trigonometric Graphs

4.5 Inverse Trigonometric Graphs

1. Horiz. Stretch by $\frac{5}{4}$

   Vert. Stretch: none

   Vert. Reflect: no

   Vert. Shift: 2 up

   Horiz. Shift: none

   Domain: $\left[-\frac{5}{4}, \frac{5}{4} \right]$

   Range: $\left[2 - \frac{\pi}{2}, 2 + \frac{\pi}{2} \right]$

2. Horiz. Shrink by $\frac{1}{3}$

   Vert. Stretch: $\frac{2}{3}$

   Vert. Reflect: no

   Vert. Shift: $\frac{4\pi}{3}$ down

   Horiz. Shift: 1 left

   Domain: $\left[-\frac{4}{3}, -\frac{2}{3} \right]$

   Range: $\left[-\frac{4\pi}{3}, -\frac{2\pi}{3} \right]$

3. Horiz. Stretch by 4

   Vert. Stretch: 2

   Vert. Reflect: yes

   Vert. Shift: none

   Horiz. Shift: 3 left

   Domain: $(-\infty, \infty)$

   Range: $(-\pi, \pi)$

4. Horiz. Shrink by $\frac{3}{4}$

   Vert. Stretch: 2

   Vert. Reflect: yes

   Vert. Shift: none

   Horiz. Shift: 3 left

   Domain: $(-\infty, \infty)$

   Range: $(-\pi, \pi)$

5. Horiz. Shrink by $\frac{1}{2}$

   Vert. Stretch: $\frac{1}{3\pi}$

   Vert. Reflect: yes

   Vert. Shift: 1 down

   Horiz. Shift: 2 right

   Domain: $\left[\frac{3}{2}, \frac{5}{2} \right]$

   Range: $\left[-\frac{7}{6}, -\frac{5}{6} \right]$

6. Horiz. Shrink by $\frac{1}{7}$

   Vert. Stretch: 3

   Vert. Reflect: no

   Vert. Shift: none

   Horiz. Shift: $\frac{4}{7}$ right

   Domain: $(-\infty, \infty)$

   Range: $\left(-\frac{3\pi}{2}, \frac{3\pi}{2} \right)$

7. Horiz. Stretch: none

   Vert. Stretch: 3

   Vert. Reflect: yes

   Vert. Shift: $\frac{7\pi}{4}$ up

   Horiz. Shift: 3 left

   Domain: $[-4, -2]$

   Range: $\left[\frac{\pi}{4}, \frac{13\pi}{4} \right]$

8. Horiz. Stretch by 4

   Vert. Stretch: 4

   Vert. Reflect: no

   Vert. Shift: 2π up

   Horiz. Shift: 4 right

   Domain: $[0, 8]$

   Range: $[2\pi, 6\pi]$

Unit 5: Applications of Trigonometry

5.1 More Inverse Trigonometry

1. $\sin^{-1}\left(-\dfrac{\sqrt{3}}{2}\right) = -\dfrac{\pi}{3}$

2. $\arctan\left(\dfrac{\sqrt{3}}{3}\right) = \dfrac{\pi}{6}$

3. $\sec^{-1}\left(-\sqrt{2}\right) = \dfrac{3\pi}{4}$

4. $\csc^{-1}(2) = \dfrac{\pi}{6}$

5. $\sin\left(\arctan\left(-\sqrt{3}\right)\right) = -\dfrac{\sqrt{3}}{2}$

6. $\cot(-\cos^{-1}(0.75) = -\dfrac{3\sqrt{7}}{7}$

7. $\tan\left(\sin^{-1}\left(\dfrac{5x-6}{7x+4}\right)\right)$
   $= \dfrac{5x-6}{\sqrt{24x^2 + 116x - 20}}$

8. $\sin\left(\sec^{-1}\left(-\dfrac{2}{x-3}\right)\right)$
   $= \dfrac{\sqrt{-x^2 + 6x - 5}}{2}$

5.2 Law of Sines

1. A=25°, B=69°, C=86°, a=7, b=15.46, c=16.52

2. A=26°, B=34°, C=120°, a=11, b=14.03, c=21.73

3. A=48°, B=46°, C=86°, a=7, b=6.78, c=9.40

4. A=92°, B=32°, C=56°, a=30.17, b=16, c=25.03

5. A=60°, B=45°, C=75°, a=8.97, b=7.32, c=10

6. A=70°, B=33°, C=77°, a=13.50, b=7.83, c=14

5.3 The Ambiguous Case

1. A=32.39°, B=26.61°, C=121°, a=10, b=8.36, c=16

2. A=72.89°, B=49°, C=58.11°, a=10.13, b=8, c=9
   A'=9.11°, B'=49°, C'=121.89°, a'=1.68, b'=8, c'=9

3. No triangle possible

4. A=80°, B=55.15°, C=44.85°, a=24, b=17.19, c=20

5. A=57.02°, B=69.98°, C=53°, a=8.93, b=10, c=8.5
   A'=16.98°, B'=110.02°, C'=53°, a'=3.11, b'=10, c'=8.5

6. A=23.53°, B=29°, C=127.47°, a=14, b=17, c=27.83

7. No triangle possible

8. A=60°, B=90°, C=30° a=15.59, b=18, c=9

Unit 5: Applications of Trigonometry

5.4 Law of Cosines

1. A=50.48°, B=58.99°, C=70.53°, a=9, b=10, c=11

2. A=36.96°, B=32.30°, C=110.74°, a=9, b=8, c=14

3. A=30.03°, B=78°, C=71.97°, a=10, b=19.54, c=19

4. A=67.97°, B=80.03°, C=32°, a=16, b=17, c=9.15

5. A=34.05°, B=23.07°, C=122.88°, a=10, b=7, c=15

6. A=137°, B=35.13°, C=7.87°, a=24.89, b=21, c=5

7. A=64.99°, B=49°, C=66.01°, a=22.82, b=19, c=23
   A'=17.01°, B'=49°, C'=113.99°, a'=7.36, b'=19, c'=23

8. A=132.89°, B=23.56°, C=23.56°, a=11, b=6, c=6

Unit 6: Trigonometric Identities

6.1 Introduction to Identities

1. a) 0.283
   b) 0.294
   c) -1.042

2. a) -1.254
   b) 0.782
   c) 1.604

3. a) $\dfrac{\sqrt{25-a^2}}{5}$

   b) $\dfrac{\sqrt{25-a^2}}{a}$

   c) $-\dfrac{5}{a}$

4. $\sin\theta$

5. 1

6. $\sec^2\beta - \tan\beta$

7. $\tan^2\theta$

8. $\tan^2 x$

9. $2\csc\theta$

6.2 Verifying Identities
Proofs are on pg. 169

6.3 Sum & Difference Identities

1. $\dfrac{\sqrt{2}-\sqrt{6}}{4}$

2. $2-\sqrt{3}$

3. $\sqrt{6}-\sqrt{2}$

4. $\dfrac{1+\tan(5x)}{\tan(5x)-1}$

5. $\dfrac{\sqrt{2}+\sqrt{6}}{4}$

6. $\dfrac{2\sqrt{82}}{9-\sqrt{3}}$

7. $\dfrac{2\sqrt{7}-3\sqrt{21}}{6+7\sqrt{3}}$

8. $\dfrac{2\sqrt{91}+21}{10\sqrt{53}}$

9. $-\dfrac{7\sqrt{6}}{12}$

10. $\cot y - \tan x$

11. $-\tan x$

12. $\tan\alpha$

6.4 Double & Half Angle Identities

1. $\dfrac{\sqrt{2}+\sqrt{6}}{4}$

2. $\dfrac{\sqrt{2}}{2-\sqrt{2}}$

3. $\dfrac{\sqrt{2+\sqrt{2}}}{2}$

4. $\dfrac{2}{\sqrt{2-\sqrt{2-\sqrt{2}}}}$

5. -2

6. $-\dfrac{\sqrt[4]{244}}{\sqrt{6+\sqrt{61}}}$

7. $\dfrac{-12\sqrt{221}-184}{23\sqrt{17}-96\sqrt{13}}$

8. $\dfrac{147\sqrt{11}}{1250}$

9. $-\dfrac{7\sqrt{39}}{195}$

10. $\sin(8a)$

11. $1+\sin w$

12. $\sin^2\theta$

Unit 6: Trigonometric Identities

6.5 Power Reducing Identities

1. $\dfrac{16}{3 + 4\cos(2x) + \cos(4x)}$

2. $\dfrac{3 + 4\cos(2x) + \cos(4x)}{1 - \cos(2x)}$

3. $6\sqrt{2} + 12$

4. $-\dfrac{\sqrt{2 - \sqrt{2}}}{2}$

5. $\dfrac{3 - 4\cos(4x) + \cos(8x)}{3 + 4\cos(4x) + \cos(8x)}$

6. $\dfrac{10 + \sqrt{19}}{20}$

7. $\dfrac{\sqrt{41} + 4}{2\sqrt{41}}$

Unit 6: Trigonometric Identities

6.2 Verifying Identities   Note: Proofs may vary.

1.

Statements	Reasons
$\dfrac{1-\sin x}{\cos x} + \dfrac{\cos x}{1+\sin x} = \dfrac{2\cos x}{1+\sin x}$	Given
$\dfrac{(1-\sin x)(1+\sin x)+(\cos x)(\cos x)}{\cos x(1+\sin x)} =$	Common Denominators
$\dfrac{1-\sin^2 x + \cos^2 x}{\cos x(1+\sin x)} =$	Difference of Squares & Simplify
$\dfrac{2\cos^2 x}{\cos x(1+\sin x)} =$	Pythagorean Identity
$\dfrac{2\cos x}{1+\sin x} = \dfrac{2\cos x}{1+\sin x}$	Simplify ▪ Q.E.D.

2.

Statements	Reasons
$\sec\theta + \tan\theta = \dfrac{\cos\theta}{1-\sin\theta}$	Given
$\dfrac{1}{\cos\theta} + \dfrac{\sin\theta}{\cos\theta} =$	Reciprocal & Quotient Identities
$\dfrac{1+\sin\theta}{\cos\theta}\left(\dfrac{1-\sin\theta}{1-\sin\theta}\right) =$	Simplify & Rewriting expression
$\dfrac{1-\sin^2\theta}{\cos\theta(1-\sin\theta)} =$	Difference of Squares
$\dfrac{\cos^2\theta}{\cos\theta(1-\sin\theta)} =$	Pythagorean Identity
$\dfrac{\cos\theta}{1-\sin\theta} = \dfrac{\cos\theta}{1-\sin\theta}$	Simplify ▪ Q.E.D.

Unit 6: Trigonometric Identities

3.

Statements	Reasons
$\cos\alpha\cot\alpha + \sin\alpha - \csc\alpha = 0$	Given
$\cos\alpha \cdot \dfrac{\cos\alpha}{\sin\alpha} + \sin\alpha - \dfrac{1}{\sin\alpha} =$	Reciprocal & Quotient Identities
$\dfrac{\cos^2\alpha + \sin^2\alpha - 1}{\sin\alpha} =$	Rewrite $\sin\alpha$ as fraction & simplify
$\dfrac{1-1}{\sin\alpha} =$	Pythagorean Identity
$0 = 0$	Simplify
	∎ Q.E.D.

4.

Statements	Reasons
$\sin(-x) = \dfrac{\sin^2 x - 1}{\csc x - \tan x \cos x}$	Given
$= \dfrac{\sin^2 x - 1}{\dfrac{1}{\sin x} - \dfrac{\sin x}{\cos x} \cdot \cos x}$	Reciprocal & Quotient Identities
$= \dfrac{\sin^2 x - 1}{\dfrac{1}{\sin x} - \sin x} \left(\dfrac{\sin x}{\sin x}\right)$	Simplify
$= \dfrac{-(1 - \sin^2 x)(\sin x)}{1 - \sin^2 x}$	Rewriting expression
$= -\sin x$	Simplify
$\sin(-x) = \sin(-x)$	Cofunction Identity
	∎ Q.E.D.

Unit 6: Trigonometric Identities

5.

Statements	Reasons
$(\tan x + 1)^2(\cot x + 1)^2 = (\sec x \csc x + 2)^2$	Given
$(\tan^2 x + 2\tan x + 1)(\cot^2 x + 2\cot x + 1) =$	Expand squared binomials
$(\sec^2 x + 2\tan x)(\csc^2 x + 2\cot x) =$	Pythagorean Identity
$\sec^2 x \csc^2 x + 2\sec^2 x \cot x$ $+2\csc^2 x \tan x + 4\cot x \tan x =$	Multiply binomials
$\sec^2 x \csc^2 x + 2\left(\dfrac{1}{\cos^2 x}\right)\left(\dfrac{\cos x}{\sin x}\right)$ $+2\left(\dfrac{1}{\sin^2 x}\right)\left(\dfrac{\sin x}{\cos x}\right) + 4\left(\dfrac{1}{\tan x}\right)\tan x =$	Reciprocal & Quotient Identities
$\sec^2 x \csc^2 x + 2\sec x \csc x$ $+2\csc x \sec x + 4 =$	Simplify
$\sec^2 x \csc^2 x + 4\sec x \csc x + 4 =$	Combine Like Terms
$(\sec x \csc x + 2)^2 = (\sec x \csc x + 2)^2$	Factor trinomial

$\blacksquare$ Q.E.D.

Unit 6: Trigonometric Identities

6.

Statements	Reasons
$$\dfrac{\csc \beta}{\tan \beta + \cot \beta} = \cos \beta$$	Given
$$\dfrac{\dfrac{1}{\sin \beta}}{\dfrac{\sin \beta}{\cos \beta} + \dfrac{\cos \beta}{\sin \beta}} \left(\dfrac{\sin \beta \cos \beta}{\sin \beta \cos \beta} \right) =$$	Reciprocal & Quotient Identities
$$\dfrac{\cos \beta}{\sin^2 \beta + \cos^2 \beta} =$$	Rewrite expression to clear denominators
$$\cos \beta = \cos \beta$$	Pythagorean Identity
	■ Q.E.D.

7.

Statements	Reasons
$$\dfrac{\tan x}{1 + \sec x} - \dfrac{1 + \sec x}{\tan x} = -2 \cot x$$	Given
$$\dfrac{\tan x (\tan x) - (1 + \sec x)^2}{\tan x (1 + \sec x)} =$$	Common Denominators
$$\dfrac{\tan^2 x - 1 - 2\sec x - \sec^2 x}{\tan x (1 + \sec x)} =$$	Expand expressions
$$\dfrac{-2 - 2\sec x}{\tan x (1 + \sec x)} =$$	Pythagorean Identity & Simplify
$$\dfrac{-2(1 + \sec x)}{\tan x (1 + \sec x)} =$$	Factor -2
$$-2 \cot x = -2 \cot x$$	Simplify & Reciprocal Identity ■ Q.E.D.

Unit 6: Trigonometric Identities

8.

Statements	Reasons
$\dfrac{\cos x \cot x}{\csc x - 1} = 1 + \sin x$	Given
$\dfrac{\cos x \cdot \frac{\cos x}{\sin x}}{\frac{1}{\sin x} - 1}\left(\dfrac{\sin x}{\sin x}\right) =$	Reciprocal & Quotient Identities
$\dfrac{\cos^2 x}{1 - \sin x} =$	Rewrite expression
$\dfrac{1 - \sin^2 x}{1 - \sin x} =$	Pythagorean Identity
$\dfrac{(1 - \sin x)(1 + \sin x)}{1 - \sin x} =$	Difference of Squares
$1 + \sin x = 1 + \sin x$	Simplify

■ Q.E.D.

9.

Statements	Reasons
$\tan^4 x + \tan^2 x = \sec^4 x - \sec^2 x$	Given
$\tan^2 x(1 + \tan^2 x) =$	Factor $\tan^2 x$
$(\sec^2 x - 1)(\sec^2 x) =$	Pythagorean Identity
$\sec^4 x - \sec^2 x = \sec^4 x - \sec^2 x$	Distributive Property

■ Q.E.D.

10.

Statements	Reasons
$\sqrt{\dfrac{\csc\theta+1}{\csc\theta-1}} = \dfrac{\cos\theta}{1-\sin\theta}$	Given
$\sqrt{\dfrac{\csc\theta+1}{\csc\theta-1}\left(\dfrac{\sin\theta}{\sin\theta}\right)} =$	Rewrite expression
$\sqrt{\dfrac{1+\sin\theta}{1-\sin\theta}\left(\dfrac{1-\sin\theta}{1-\sin\theta}\right)} =$	Rewrite expression
$\sqrt{\dfrac{1-\sin^2\theta}{(1-\sin\theta)^2}} =$	Difference of Squares
$\sqrt{\dfrac{\cos^2\theta}{(1-\sin\theta)^2}} =$	Pythagorean Identity
$\dfrac{\cos\theta}{1-\sin\theta} = \dfrac{\cos\theta}{1-\sin\theta}$	Simplify square root

■ Q.E.D.

Notes

Notes

Notes

A GUIDE TO
THE WORLD OF
HIGH SCHOOL
TRIGONOMETRY

Made in United States
Orlando, FL
05 April 2025

60179201R00103